Happy Birthday
Gillian

~~Love~~
Just Say
NooooooVooooo!

X X x

& love

I SAID NO THANKS

I SAID
NO THANKS

THE AUTOBIOGRAPHY

NACHO NOVO

WITH DARRELL KING

BLACK & WHITE PUBLISHING

First published 2010
by Black & White Publishing Ltd
29 Ocean Drive, Edinburgh EH6 6JL

3 5 7 9 10 8 6 4 2   10 11 12 13

ISBN: 978 1 84502 286 0

Typeset by Ellipsis Books Limited, Glasgow
Printed and bound by MPG Books Ltd, Bodmin, Cornwall

CONTENTS

DEDICATION

I want to dedicate this book to the memory of my wonderful mother, Isabel, who left this world too early six years ago. There is not a day goes past I don't think about her.

To my sister Arantxa; to Donna, Dylan, Ross and Javier – you all mean the world to me.

Nacho Novo

ACKNOWLEDGEMENTS

I'd like to thank everyone at Black & White Publishing for their patience and understanding throughout this project. To the fans of Rangers Football Club for the past six years – you have been 'Simply the Best'. To Graeme Park for being a loyal friend at all times and helping us get the book off and running.

Finally, to Darrell. Thanks pal, for all the hours you put in, for being there and doing a fantastic job.

Nacho Novo

To Campbell, Alison, Janne and all the team at Black & White Publishing – your support when things got tough was really appreciated. Thanks to SNS pictures, everyone at the *Evening Times* and to GP. A good friend, critic, and fountain of knowledge. To Shannon for keeping me going.

Finally, to Nacho . . . I told you we would get there!

Darrell King

FOREWORD
BY WALTER SMITH MBE

I have worked with some special foreign talents over my two spells as manager of Rangers Football Club, but scarcely have I come across a more passionate and infectious character than Nacho Novo.

I admit to having been a little unsure of him when I returned to Rangers in January 2007 for my second tenure – but I quickly realised that there are not too many players in the game like him. One minute he can be infuriatingly erratic and the next he will produce something quite extraordinary. I am pleased to say I have experienced more of the latter than the former.

Of course, it has not been to Nacho's liking that he has regularly been used as a substitute as he would like to start every game. However, there have been few players in the Scottish game more capable of changing a game when called upon.

Nacho is a one-off really; although we should actually say 'there are only two Nacho Novos' as at times he can be brilliant, and at other times very frustrating! He is one of these boys who display such great natural enthusiasm for the game and he is a player that the Rangers supporters love for that trait. He is very much one of their favourites and that adulation is only reserved for those who earn it. Nacho has done that in their eyes.

He scores fantastic goals, he goes on fantastic runs, but on other occasions he can do something completely frustrating! But we love him for what he is, and that's why we enjoy working with him.

He is a fantastic substitute – although I know he doesn't like that tag because he wants to play in the team the same as anybody else – as he always has an impact on the game. It's not to his liking when he starts games on the bench but you always get a spark from him when he is introduced.

There are a number of players in the modern game who imply their affinity to a certain club when there is clearly no depth of feeling. However, when Nacho kisses the badge or salutes the Rangers fans they know he means it. Nacho really wears his heart on his sleeve, he loves his football and he is a pleasure to work with.

I used to think he was erratic in what he did, but now I just appreciate that he has his own style. He is what he is and you are never going to change him or want to change him. He always wants to play more than I have picked him and I always appreciate that and that it can affect him a bit.

Nacho is one of these lads who get a wee bit downhearted when he is not picked but as soon as he gets onto that pitch you would never know that. It's simply because he cares, which is a trait very welcome in the modern game.

Nacho has also been at the heart of Rangers' greatest triumphs since I returned and I will always be indebted to him for his contributions and his role in helping the club win trophies over the recent period.

He has scored vital goals at home and in Europe, goals that no Rangers fan will ever forget. That is something not too many players can say. He should be proud of that, of what he has done and the place he has written for himself in the Rangers' history books.

He has been terrific for us on the big stage and he has scored some really important goals – none more so than the penalty in Florence that took us to the UEFA Cup Final in 2008 in Manchester.

It was an incredible moment when he stepped up to take that last spot kick against Fiorentina in the second leg of the semi-final and it is one none of us are liable to forget. I was quite content when it was Nacho going up to take the decisive kick. I knew the stage was set for him.

It was the same in the Scottish Cup Final last season against Falkirk when we introduced him at half-time from the bench and he produced one of the great Hampden Park winning goals from forty-five yards with his first kick to help the team clinch the domestic double. That is Nacho Novo. He will always have a place in the heart of every Rangers fan.

1

I SAID NO THANKS

The voice on the other end of the phone delivered the state-ment that was about to send my already turbulent summer into a complete head-spin.

He said: 'Hi Nacho, it's Peter Lawwell here. We would like to talk to you about joining Celtic.'

You could have knocked me over with a feather. I muttered a reply about him having to speak to my agent first and then ended the conversation. I sat there in my house in Broughty Ferry and stared into space. Where was this situation going now?

I had clung on for weeks to my dream of leaving Dundee for Glasgow – but to sign for Rangers, not their arch-rivals.

Now, as Rangers and Dundee failed to strike a deal, my agent, Jorge Leira, was taking a call from the club – just minutes after the one I had from Peter Lawwell – to say that Dundee had agreed a fee for me with Celtic and I was free to talk to them. I could hardly take in what I was hearing.

There have been many theories about my huge desire to sign for Rangers and before I go into what happened with the whole Celtic situation, I think it's important to clear up exactly where the roots of that came from.

When I moved to Huesca in the summer of 2000, I shared

1

a flat with the captain of the team, Guillermo Mingarro. He was a really good guy who liked to travel around Europe on holiday in the close season. Everywhere he went, he would pick up a football strip from whatever team, or teams, were based in the city he was staying in. Mingarro had visited Scotland and had bought a Rangers top a few years before. It was the blue Adidas one with the three stripes worn in the mid-90s by top players like Paul Gascoigne and Brian Laudrup. The one he had had a number nine on the back – no name as that wasn't the done thing back then – although I was to discover later that this was the strip made famous by Ally McCoist, Rangers' finest ever striker.

One day in the flat Mingarro gave the strip to me. I had no idea who Rangers were; in fact I thought it was an American Ice Hockey or baseball top because of the name 'Rangers'.

Mingarro told me they were a famous team in Scotland and from there the name just stuck in my mind. A year or so later, I was watching TV when some highlights came on of Henrik Larsson. He had just finished an amazing season at Celtic, scoring well over forty goals. They had an interview with him and they cut into it with some goals against Rangers. The blue strip caught my eye and that was basically how it all started.

Of course, when I was offered the chance to move to Scotland, to Raith Rovers, I knew all about Rangers and Celtic as I had followed the league for a while since becoming an unofficial 'fan' with my blue strip!

I became very friendly with Mikel Arteta, a fellow Spaniard who was at Rangers and he used to get me tickets to go to some of the games. I went to a couple of games at Ibrox and also sat in the Rangers End at Hampden with Mikel's girlfriend, his dad and agent when he played in the 2-1 League Cup win over Celtic in 2003. I loved that experience and I felt that the Rangers fans were the best in the world.

So it was from there that my desire to play for Rangers had begun. In the January transfer window of 2004 there had been a lot of speculation that Rangers wanted me. My head was spinning at the thought but I never heard anything concrete from the club about trying to sign me, although I had heard that their manager, Alex McLeish, liked me as a player.

My late mother, Isabel, was staying with me in Scotland on holiday when the news hit the press that Rangers were interested in me.

We spoke about it and she said to me: 'You will sign for them one day, son. If you want something enough, and play with your heart every time you go on the pitch, then you will be a Rangers player.' I always held those words true.

When Rangers did make an approach for me in June 2004, I could hardly contain my excitement. I had returned for pre-season with Dundee and knew that, given the financial problems at Dens Park, they would let me go if the money was right. Before the offer from Ibrox came in, I spoke with one of the club's owners, Peter Marr, and told him that I wanted to be given the chance to further my career if the right move was there. In my mind, the only move that would be for me was Rangers.

Dundee had signed me for £100,000 and my understanding of the figure that they wanted for me was £500,000, which was not a bad return after the two decent years I had given the club and which I'd certainly enjoyed. But that's where the problems started with Rangers. They did not have the money of the past and every penny had to be accounted for now.

The clubs had reached an impasse and I was left in limbo.

My agent, Jorge, more or less moved in with me. We sat by the phone every day after training waiting for news as Rangers and Dundee haggled over a fee. It was a very stressful time as my whole future was on the line. Jorge tried to keep me calm, told me to stay patient, as these things had a tendency to sort themselves out, given time.

But it was mental torture. There was even chat that Rangers would wait until the following January, try to sign me on a pre-contract and then I would move to Glasgow on a Bosman free transfer when my deal expired at Dens Park in the summer of 2005.

I think that maybe came out to apply a bit of pressure on Dundee, as they had to get some money in for me. If they thought Rangers would back away, and if I dug in, then they might get nothing and be left with an unhappy player on their hands for a whole season, and a player who they had to pay when he was obviously not going to be committed to the cause. Something had to give, I thought.

I had no direct contact with anyone at Rangers and just left any conversations that were going on between all the parties to Jorge. Then, right out of nowhere, I took the call from Peter Lawwell.

I knew Celtic were a huge club. We had played against them in my two years at Dundee and they had a fantastic stadium and some very good players. The manager, Martin O'Neill, had delivered great success, including taking them to the UEFA Cup Final in 2003 which they had lost to Porto. But they had won league titles and were being more successful than Rangers.

That said, in my opinion, Rangers were the better club. I

4

looked at Rangers right from the very start of that summer as my only option. I just did not want to join anyone else.

Jorge took another phone call from Peter Marr as he tried to persuade him that I should go to Glasgow and talk to Celtic and see what they had to offer. Out of courtesy, I agreed. Myself and Jorge made plans to travel to Parkhead to meet the Celtic hierarchy, even though there was not one thought in my mind that I would sign for them. It was 29 June by this time.

There were some photographers when we arrived at Parkhead. I got pictured going in the front door of the stadium with Jorge and I listened on the radio as the sports bulletins said that Celtic were about to steal me from right under the noses of Rangers, who had been chasing me for about three weeks at this stage.

Upon entering the ground, we went to talk with Martin O'Neill and Peter Lawwell. I never said much as we got a tour of the trophy room and the stadium itself. I then went to O'Neill's office and we talked a bit about the season that had just finished and football in general. Jorge spoke more with Peter Lawwell.

As I got up to leave O'Neill's office – and I have to say I found him a very good guy, the kind of manager who has presence when you meet him for the first time – he playfully grabbed me around the neck with both hands and said: 'You better sign for us, wee man.'

They knew that Rangers were in for me big time. No matter how small it may be to the outside world, the Old Firm loved nothing better – they still do – than getting one up on each other. If I had signed for Celtic it would have been a major slap in the face for Rangers as the financial gap was only around £50,000 between what they had offered and what Dundee wanted.

We never talked about personal terms with Celtic. We never talked about length of contract. I was very subdued and I think that was the reason they later said they would not be pursuing the deal, as I had not shown any enthusiasm. That was right; I didn't want to sign for Celtic. I was never going to do it. We parted, said thanks, and it was left that we would stay in touch. Jorge and I never said much in the car on the way back to Dundee. He knew my mind. He knew it had to be Rangers. But something had to give.

Every day just seemed to take an eternity and there were times when I just felt that it would never happen. It can be hard when you want something so much, you feel close to it, but not close enough to actually get there. That was how I felt every day of that summer. Of course, I was not happy with Dundee about this situation. In my mind, they should have taken the money from Rangers and let me go. Of course, I was only seeing it from one side of things. They were looking out for the club and its best interests, but from a player's angle you never really see it that way. There was a lot of talking going on and I knew it had to come to a head.

Jorge and I were called to another meeting at Dens Park with Peter Marr. I felt that it was time to force the issue as much as I could.

Peter already knew that he was wasting his breath trying to talk me into going anywhere else. Celtic, by this time, had gone public that they would not be pursuing me any more due to how I had acted at Parkhead when I had arrived. There was some interest from other clubs in England and a couple in Spain, but Peter knew that it was Rangers or nothing.

We sat in the office at Dens Park, me directly across from Peter with Jorge sitting on a chair over against the wall. I could tell right away that Peter was bristling. I liked him. He had always been a good man, but as far as I was concerned he was the guy blocking my dream move to Rangers. We were going at it and voices began to get raised.

'So you won't sell me to Rangers, fine then. I will stay at Dundee and not go anywhere,' I shouted at Peter. 'But I can tell you this. I won't play for you. Every day, my knee will be f——. It will be too sore for me to train and play. That's the way it will be. This is my career, my life and I want you to sell me to Rangers – no-one else.'

Peter flew into a fit of rage. To be fair, what I was saying was out of order, but I was trying to think of anything I could to force Dundee's hand. And, as Jorge cowered in the corner, I told him again there was no way I would play for Dundee.

Peter screamed back at me: 'You are refusing to play now? You are refusing to play? Well, there you go, you can get what you want. Go to Rangers.'

He stood up, leaned down and scribbled his signature on the paper that granted me permission to talk to Rangers. And then he shouted: 'Now get out of my face.'

I got up and quickly left the scene. God knows what Jorge thought of what he had just witnessed. It was hardly a calm sight but I found a chair in the corridor and just took a seat. Jorge stayed inside to finalise things with Peter and I just shut my eyes and tried to get my breath back. I had just heard what I wanted. I could go and sign for Rangers.

It was maybe only ten minutes that Jorge and Peter stayed in there talking, probably just enough time for Peter to calm down.

Looking back on it, he was absolutely right to take the stance he did for as long as he did. He had to put the interests of Dundee first. I just felt that it was time to meet in the middle a bit as no-one was going to win.

The office door opened and Peter came out followed by Jorge. He walked over to me and I stood up. Peter gave me a cuddle and said: 'You have the chance you want now, son. Good luck and thanks for your efforts for this club.'

That meant a lot to me. I had given Dundee everything. They had been good for me and provided me with the chance to play at a higher level. But I was not one of these foreign players who can come to a club and never try to make a bond with the people and the fans. I had given Peter Marr and Jimmy Marr, his brother and co-owner, everything. I had given everything to Jim Duffy, the manager. And the fans had always been very good with me. I always did my very best for Dundee and loved being there, but I'm a footballer and a man with many ambitions and this was Rangers. It was my dream. I didn't know, if it hadn't come off, if there would be another chance to sign for them in the future. Now, after one final argument, I was on my way.

With permission granted, Jorge and I headed for Glasgow once again to speak to Rangers. It was 6 July, one week after I had travelled the same road for my talks with Celtic. I was very nervous on the way down from Dundee. It was such a big move for me and I just wanted to get there and get things done. Driving into Murray Park was an amazing feeling.

As the gates opened and we went in I just looked around and thought 'wow'. It was an amazing complex looking at it for the first time, a far cry from anything I had ever seen at Raith and Dundee. With these kinds of facilities, everything was there for a player to train in top conditions and be well looked after.

We went inside and Jorge headed off to talk with Martin Bain about my personal terms. I then had my first conversation with Alex McLeish. He said: 'It's taken a bit of time, wee man. But at last you're here!'

I was delighted to hear that from him. It showed faith in me right away. It felt good that Alex McLeish had kept Rangers' interest alive when they could have walked away when Dundee blocked it. He needed players in, the season was not far away from starting, and he could have looked elsewhere. But he had stayed on my trail. That meant a lot to me.

I went off for a medical and left Jorge to complete the terms on a four-year contract. Signing that piece of paper was the best moment of my life. I looked down, saw the Rangers badge on the top of the documents and just felt so happy. Everything I had worked for, my dreams of getting to a top club. With one signature, I was there. Nacho Novo, of Glasgow Rangers.

There was a bit of sadness that I couldn't rush out the door and call my mum. I knew she would have been up there looking over me and smiling as we had talked so many times about my hopes of becoming a Rangers player one day.

We had a signing conference and I was unveiled to the press. Alex McLeish made a joke that I was so small I could 'run under a table with a top hat on', but it was just the best feeling ever. I met all my new teammates and saw some of the quality players I would be sharing a dressing room with every day. The good thing was that I was one of a number of new signings, so there were other people trying to find their feet, not just me. But the club did everything and helped me out. One of the legendary Rangers players of the past, Sandy Jardine, works as a player liaison and he helped with all the personal stuff you need to arrange.

I knew that, after saying no thanks to Celtic, the Rangers fans would take to me. But I had to prove myself to them, show that I could score goals at Rangers after doing it at Dundee. I also knew that I had alienated one half of the city because of my decision not to move to Parkhead. These were the issues I would have to deal with. But I was where I wanted to be – at Rangers.

2

GROWING UP IN GALICIA

Ignacio Javier Gomez Novo was never a hard kid to identify on the streets of Caranza, a tough working class suburb in the town of Ferrol, Galicia. I was either kicking a ball – or getting into trouble and driving my parents, Ricardo and Isabel, absolutely crazy.

My passion for football was something that had been drummed into me from a very early age by my father, himself an accomplished professional player who enjoyed more than a decent career in Spain. Dad was a big, aggressive central defender who loved a tackle. He took no prisoners and played with his heart on his sleeve, a trait I was to inherit later in life when my own career began in earnest.

My father was my idol. From the first time I ran around kicking the ball I wanted to be him.

As for my mother, we always had a very special bond. We were very close, and she spent all of her time outside of her own sporting career as a semi-professional basketball player looking after me from the moment I arrived on March 26, 1979, and then when my sister, Arantxa, came along six years later.

Ferrol was a good town. The people were honest as the day was long. The mainstay of the community, the Navantia

11

shipbuilding yards, was where a huge section of the popu-
lation earned a living. Sure, it had tough parts. Caranza wasn't
exactly a plush, leafy, well-to-do area and you had to be
streetwise. There were dangerous roads young people could
have gone down had they chosen the wrong path, with alcohol,
drugs, violence and theft all very much problems for the
community.

Thankfully, for me, my parents drove me on. They knew I
had a chance to make the grade in football as my youth career
developed and they were determined to keep me on the
straight and narrow – not that they always succeeded!

My early recollections of life centre on my dad's career.
Whilst we always had a home in Ferrol, much of my early
childhood was nomadic as we moved around following my
dad's transfers to different clubs.

He had started out with Racing Ferrol, his hometown club.
They were not the biggest team in the region by any stretch
– the Amalata Stadium housing around 12,000 fans – and they
spent most of their time flirting between Segunda Division
and Segunda Division B, the two tiers below the Primera Liga
top flight.

But my dad's career had taken off quite quickly, and before
long Real Betis targeted him. The Novo family, with myself
just a baby, were off to Sevilla, a beautiful town with a proud
footballing tradition and fierce inter-city rivalry between Betis
and Sevilla.

My dad was a good friend of Rafael Gordillo, who was a
mainstay of the Betis team and a player who was to go on to
become one of Spain's finest ever defenders. He was capped
seventy-five times for his country and after nine years at Betis
moved to Real Madrid where he stayed for a further seven

years, forming a formidable full-back partnership with himself on the left and Jose Camacho on the right. We stayed in Gordillo's flat while we looked for a house in Sevilla and I became quite close to him.

Many years after he baby-sat me, Gordillo took me to meet one of the finest ever strikers to have come out of Spain. Emilio Butragueno – or 'The Vulture' as he became known because of his predatory instincts in the penalty box – had been a teammate of his at the Bernabeau for many seasons.

We went to see Butragueno the night before Madrid faced Deportivo in La Coruna. When I walked into the room I expected to see this star player maybe sitting back thinking he was king of all around him. Instead, Butragueno had his nose in a pile of books. He looked up from them as we came in, closed them over and began to talk to me after Gordillo had made the introductions. I told him that my dream was to be a famous striker, just like him, to play for Real Madrid and also Spain.

He smiled at me. I'll never forget his words. 'Concentrate on your studies, that is the most important thing for you to always remember,' said The Vulture.

I nodded my head. I was awe-struck at even being in the same room as this legend. But to be honest it was never advice that I followed. Clearly, education was important to him. And, when he finished playing, he went on to become the Sporting Director at Madrid, which proves he was a very intelligent guy whose brains weren't just in his boots.

My father was doing well at Betis and attracted interest from Espanyol, but just as the basis of a transfer was beginning to be formulated, disaster struck. He tore his cruciate knee ligament in a game and the deal was off. That was a shattering blow as, back then, recovery from that kind of injury was far longer than now. Indeed, many players failed to ever come back from a cruciate problem.

Dad, as was his way, battled hard to get his career back on track. His next move, though, was not to the bright lights of Barcelona where Espanyol play but to Lorca, who were based in Murcia. I was around three years old by then. And one of the first things the Novo family did on arrival was to send the town into a frenzy over a missing child!

My mother and father had gone out for a meal at a local restaurant, leaving me in the capable hands of a babysitter. But I was always up to something. I could never sit in the one place and even at that age I had a sense for devilment. When the girl wasn't looking I slipped out the back door of the house and escaped out the back garden. As you could imagine, she was frantic when she couldn't find me after searching the house upstairs and down.

Now I was quite a distinctive kid as I had very long hair – we had only been in Lorca for a short while but people had got to know me in the neighbourhood. The girl was beside herself as time wore on. After enlisting the help of some people from the street she knew it was time to phone my mum and dad. They got the call halfway through their meal that I had gone missing. Naturally they were frantic, fearing I had been snatched or I had injured myself somewhere after getting lost.

They raced back to the house and by this time the local Polizia were on the scene asking the girl, who was now in floods of tears, what had happened, when was the last time she had seen me, what I was wearing. A full-scale search was launched. Everyone was racing around the area asking passers by if they had seen a little kid with long hair, going by the name of Nacho, as he had gone missing.

Around 3km from our house a circus had rolled into town for a few days and many of the locals were attending that night. My dad raced down and asked to speak to the organisers, just in case an appeal could be put around the crowd to ask if anyone had seen me.

By this time my mother was beside herself. She knew that I was always a cocky little guy, but the thought of a three-year-old roaming the streets – or something more sinister – had her struggling to keep it together.

Inside, dad was losing it as well. But he knew that he had to try and stay positive. That became harder, though, when the promoter in charge of the circus came out and told my parents they hadn't seen any kids running around and no-one had passed a lost child in to the security office. Now, as darkness was coming in, it was beginning to get extremely serious.

Just as my parents were ready to head off and continue the search elsewhere, one of the workers from the circus came out and asked them to hurry inside. They were led through the back and into an area where they could see the whole arena. On the front row, squeezed in, was the longhaired kid that had caused so much worry. I had gone out the back door of the house and been drawn to the tent where all the music and noise was coming from.

And, as they pounded the streets, as the police went into full search mode, I had been sat in the very front row of the circus watching the clowns and all the animals, laughing my head off.

Let's just say my mum and dad weren't amused. But it was one of those times when they just hugged me tight and closed their eyes in sheer relief. They should have maybe then realised that life for me was not going to be dull.

And when we moved on to Marbella, the next stop of my dad's career, the mishaps just kept on coming. I was around five years old then. And mischief was at the centre of just about everything I did.

We would spend a lot of time in Puerto Banus, which is just up the road from Marbella and is one of the most exclusive areas of Spain. The port itself is a fantastic place to hang out – today it remains one of the most popular haunts in the area – with loads of bars and restaurants along the front. My dad used to go there a lot as Gordillo had a huge yacht moored in Banus and we would all go and spend days in the sun just chilling out. For me, that wasn't enough. And my love of adventure was to bring me face to face with a very dangerous beast!

There was a caravan that had been brought onto the dock for extra accommodation alongside the owner's boat. While everyone was out on the deck of Gordillo's cruiser having lunch and talking, I decided to sneak off and climb onto the roof of this caravan. I was jumping up and down for a minute or so before I realised that the skylight underneath me was about to give way. It was too late. One jump too far took me crashing through into the caravan below with an almighty noise that had everyone on the boat jumping.

The drop wasn't that big and I wasn't badly injured – but as I sat up, there I was face to face with the owner's Doberman dog.

It was a surreal moment. I sat there staring at it – and the Doberman just looked right through me. Normally, given that he'd had such a fright with a kid dropping in through the roof, it would have been in the dog's nature to react and maybe bite out. But as the people outside frantically tried to get the door open to get me out, he just sat there oblivious. As I was dragged out of the caravan door my parents shook their heads in tandem.

Marbella, it seemed, was to bring the worst out in young Nacho. The next incident again involved my high jinks – but this time I didn't get so lucky. My dad had a bar just off the front that he liked to go to for a beer in the afternoons and he got very friendly with the owner and the crowd. In Spain, some of the best social gatherings occur at these wee bars that populate most towns, with the all too frequent sight of the locals sitting there sipping coffee or a beer discussing the ills and problems of the world – and more often than not football, such is the passion for the game in Spain. Everyone has a team; everyone has an opinion or a gripe!

I would hang around with my ball while my dad got deep into conversation. As usual, boredom set in. Next to the bar there was a construction site as a new block of flats was being built. The walls and floors were in place, but there were no windows in yet. I noticed some local kids darting around inside and having a good time. It was too much for me to resist.

Within a couple of minutes I was inside the block, clambering up the ladders from floor to floor. I had watched the kids getting up to as high as the third floor then throwing themselves out and landing on the huge pile of sand that lay below.

What I hadn't factored in was that these kids were older than me, maybe seven or eight. They could spring further and make the target of the sandpit without any problem. I took a few steps back and began my run up to the open front of the building that would lead me to the sandpit. But I didn't have enough power to launch myself far enough forward. And down I came with a thump.

As we sat in the hospital looking at the plaster cast that encased my broken leg, my dad was once again left shaking his head. It was to be a recurring theme as my nose for danger, and for excitement, kept leading me into trouble.

I had started school in Marbella at this stage but my broken leg meant I was off class. It wasn't the most severe of breaks, but they told me I would have to keep the plaster on for the required length of time and stick closely to the rehabilitation plan.

To pass my days, dad would take me down to training at Marbella and I'd sit at the side of the pitch watching the players go through their paces every day.

My leg was healing. The check-ups revealed the bone was close to knitting and the cast had been changed to a slightly lighter one. The doctor, though, had told me to be careful, as this was now the final stage of the bone healing. Most kids would have been happy that they were close to freedom again. But, as usual, I had to take matters into my own hands.

One day, while I was watching yet another Marbella training session, I noticed some kids playing a small-sided game on another pitch alongside the first-team squad. My cast was getting pretty loose and worn. So, with all my strength, I tore and tore until it started to crack. Inside a minute or so the cast was off and my leg could breathe again.

Off I went to take part in the game, unaware that I was causing damage, as things had not healed properly. Like any bone break, it takes the required amount of time, and then maybe a bit extra just to be sure.

My dad was going crazy when he spotted me. He charged over and screamed to ask what I was playing at. We were quickly back at the hospital and I was told in no uncertain terms that I could have seriously risked the bone's healing process and given myself major problems. As a kid, the bones were not fully formed and the last thing I needed after a broken leg at such a young age was to be running around and causing all sorts of movement.

By now I think my dad was on first name terms with most of the people in the Marbella hospital. But the most serious of all my accidents on the Malaga coast was still to come.

We attended the wedding of my parents' friends a few months later. It was a traditional Spanish affair and, along with the other kids there, I was having a great time. Whilst the adults ate, drank and danced we were allowed to run around the grounds of the hotel and do what we wanted.

A game of tag started and we were all having fun. But it just had to be me. As I lunged forward to try and grab one of the other kids he skipped out of the way and I fell towards a wooden plywood wall panel on the side of a garden outhouse that was in the grounds of the hotel.

Normally, that kind of fall would not result in anything more serious than a grazed hand or knee. But the angle I fell at caused me to reach out and try to break the fall. My right arm crashed straight through the panel that was old, and very brittle. I screamed out in agony as blood started gushing everywhere. As the panel had shattered, one of the jagged edges from a bit that had remained connected to the house ripped right through the inside of my right arm.

19

To this day I still have the scar to remind me of the forty-two stitches, but the most fortunate thing of all, as the doctors told my parents as they again stitched me up, was that the cut had stopped just short of the main artery in my wrist. Had that been severed, chances are I would have lost blood so quickly it could have been life threatening.

Given the episodes I had been involved in during our time in Marbella, it was maybe a relief for the family when we again moved on. Dad did finally get the chance to play in the city of Barcelona, but not with Espanyol, as he would have done had injury not robbed him of the opportunity. Instead, it was with Tarrasa, again a side which operated in the lower reaches of Spanish football's four-division system, who were based in the Catalan capital. That was as far as his career went, but I had been given my first glimpses of life as a professional footballer and from then on it was all I would pursue.

The 'Os Amigos' team, part of the youth set-up at Racing, provided me with my first steps on the road. Now back in Ferrol, and with my sister also part of the Novo family by this time, it was all systems go for me as I chased the dream. I progressed through the ranks at a fair rate of knots, my speed and agility and eye for goal something that most of the coaches began to identify in me early on – along with my fiery nature.

I hated losing. I would shout and swear if things went wrong. I was down on myself as well. I found it hard to find any kind of perspective on a game, to take the good with the bad. I just wanted to win. All the time.

The 'Os Amigos' programme was good and the coaching was something I enjoyed. Things didn't go so well, however, when in a practice game I broke the leg of one of the Racing director's sons.

Studies meant nothing to me. I was well into my mid-teens at that point and I just wanted to play football. Racing were very keen to keep me in their set-up, but I was sent out to join a team called Obal, who played in the Galician regional divisions. In my first season there I scored forty-two goals. It was decision time for Racing as my eighteenth birthday was closing in and I wanted to make a decision on where my future would lie.

In 1997 I signed a professional contract with Racing Ferrol for four years. There had been rumours of interest in me from Celta Vigo and Deportivo La Coruna, but my hometown club stepped in and I signed happily.

One of the first decisions they made was to farm me out to their feeder club, UD Somozas, who played in the Tercera Division, the bottom rung of the four leagues in Spain.

I trained every day with Racing, but would go and play at the weekends for Somozas against the likes of Barcelona and Real Madrid's B teams. In Spain the vast majority of La Liga clubs have B teams who will play down the divisions. It is a chance for their promising young players to get tested at a competitive level, so the standard of player I was coming up against more often than not was very decent.

Those two seasons at Somozas proved to be crucial in my development. I quickly had to adapt to the step up from regional boys games to a higher level, even if it was in the basement of the top flight.

By the end of the 1998/99 season, I found myself at a bit of a crossroads. Again there were rumours of an interest in me from various big clubs and I was beginning to make a name for myself in the region with the amount of goals that I had been scoring.

I went to see the Racing Ferrol president. I had two years left on my contract and wanted to be involved in the first-team, but his choice was to again send me out to another club. This time it was to be to Huesca, who also played in the Tercera Division, but who were a far bigger club than Somozas.

I agreed an initial deal for a year, with a salary of around 1200 euros a month. But the president at Racing wanted a clause written into the contracts that I would not be allowed to go up and play in the Segunda Division B should Huesca get promotion that season. I think his reasoning behind that was that Racing were in that division and he didn't want me playing against them, should I stay on at Huesca, and also down to the fact that he was trying to keep me off the radar of interested parties.

The whole issue almost came to a head in my first season as a Huesca player. We finished second in the league, and went into a mini play-off against the clubs who had finished third, fourth and fifth for the right to win promotion.

Had Huesca gone up, I knew that I would be looking for another club the following season, or heading back to Racing. But after a superb league season that saw us finish second, we lost in the play-offs.

That removed any obstacle to me playing in Segunda Division B and, with my wages doubled to 2500 euros a month, I was happy to sign on again for another season at Huesca.

My future was now coming under my control, rather than Racing's. I was into the last year of my deal and they had to make a decision on what they wanted to do. Nothing came

forward in terms of a new deal right away, so I was happy
to begin another campaign with Huesca and see if I could
help them go one better than the year before.

I found the form of my life so far in the season 2000/01,
scoring thirty-eight goals for Huesca and helping them to
finish fifth in the table and secure another play-off place.
Again, there were six matches to negotiate to earn promotion
– but this time we made it and I scored in four of the six
games to help Huesca up to Segunda Division B for the first
time in five years.

But, at twenty-two years old, I had some big decisions to
make on where my next step lay – and some unexpected
offers began to emerge.

Racing had not come forward with a new contract and I
started to feel that it might well be time to sever the ties.
Castellon and Logranes were very interested in me, which
would have meant staying in Spain. And, with some of the
troubles that had kicked-off in my home life, that sounded
like a very good option.

By this point there had been problems for a while between
my mum and dad. Not what myself or Arantxa felt were
major things, but kids very rarely see the full picture when
a relationship is breaking down and you just kind of get
shielded from marital problems by your parents. Given my
respect for my dad – and my love for my mother – maybe I
just blanked out what was happening but there were big cracks
beginning to show that would eventually rip our family unit
apart.

My mum had been working as a cleaner part-time now,
and my dad had a job down in the docks. But they were split-
ting up. Dad had found someone else in his life and moved

23

out. This had been going on for a few months, but the hardest part for my mum, and the two of us in the house, was that he was still around quite a lot seeing what was happening, visiting us – and then he would go.

This devastated my mother. And my sister and me. My father had been everything to me; my absolute idol and I had based my life on following in his footsteps, making him proud. Now, as far as I was concerned, he was causing havoc with his actions. He was destroying our family and, even though I maybe didn't know the full story, what I saw was enough.

It was a horrible time. My sister was only sixteen, I was trying to get the next stage of my career sorted out and the house was in turmoil. My family meant everything to me and it broke my heart to see the state my mother had got into. She stopped eating through the stress of the marriage break-up and became anorexic. One day, when I came in from training, I walked into the living room and she was lying on the floor with a knife. She was threatening to take her own life.

I could not believe my eyes. My mum. This beautiful woman who had been a rock for her kids, who had always put us first, reduced to this. Her rake-like figure on the ground, screaming that she didn't want to go on. I slapped my mum across the face to try and get her out of whatever trance she was in. I pulled the knife away and threw it to the side, then just cradled her in my arms. It was absolute hell to see her in this condition.

So, quite quickly, huge resentment began to build inside of me towards my dad. I blamed him for what had happened and there were things he started doing that just added to my mum's stress.

I know it wasn't an easy situation for anyone, break-ups never are, but he didn't handle it the right way and he caused her so much pain. With all of this to contend with my head was spinning when I took a call from the agent I had joined up with, Lasaosa Augustin, who had a very interesting proposal.

'I have a team abroad who want to take you on trial with a view to signing you, Nacho,' came the cryptic offer.

Playing abroad was always something I had hoped to do. But it was never something I imagined would come my way so quickly.

'The team is called Raith Rovers, they play in Scotland and if you want to come you need to be in Madrid tomorrow for us to talk it over.'

I was aware of Scotland, and the two biggest teams, Rangers and Celtic, and my friend David Fernandez had already headed over to play at Airdrie. Jorge Zoco was the other player that Lasaosa had been offered the chance to fly over.

He explained to us that videos had been sent over to Raith's manager, Peter Hetherston, and that he wanted to see us training for a week before making a decision.

I immediately talked things over with my mum and my sister. They were both very excited for me and urged me to take the gamble and go. At the back of my own mind was the fact I would have to leave the two women in my life just when they needed me most. I'll never forget the strength they both showed. Our family was struggling to cope with the fall-out from my dad leaving and there was a lot of anger, most of it still burning inside me.

They told me to go. Mum said: 'Son, this is your dream. Go and chase it. Do it for me.' I went to my bedroom and cried. I loved her so much, but I would have to go. And she knew it.

The next day I travelled to Madrid and met up with Jorge Zoco and Lasaosa for our trip to Scotland. The following morning we were on an early flight to Edinburgh and my life was to change forever.

I never discussed anything about my adventure with my dad. In fact, it was to be eight long years – and much more agony later – before I managed to find it within myself to speak to him again.

3

FERROL TO FIFE

A mixture of nerves and excitement occupied my thoughts as we made the car journey from Edinburgh Airport to Kirkcaldy.

What was going on back home? How would mum and Arantxa handle me leaving for a foreign country? Would mum be able to continue her steady recovery from the personal problems that had flared up and taken her to some dark places?

They both had been used to me not being around every day when I had signed for Huesca two years before and gone to stay in Zaragoza.

But Huesca was just a forty-five minute flight away, or a few hours on the train or by car for them to come and visit or for me to go home. For all three of us, those couple of years had not really felt like me leaving home as I was back and forth so much.

Such was my concern for them both, it was hard to block it out and focus on the job in hand, which was making the next step in my career with a team I'd never heard of, or heading back to Spain.

It was a gamble for me. I knew people back home had looked at me heading to a league abroad and probably felt I wouldn't be able to cut it, but I was determined to prove the doubters wrong. Deep down, I believed in my ability. Now was the time to shine.

I knew very little about Raith Rovers. My agents had given Jorge and me some background information about the club, the set-up of the leagues in Scotland, and what we could expect.

Raith already had a Spanish player in the squad, Alvaro Tejero, a left back, and I had talked with him about life in Scotland.

David Fernandez, whom I had come to know from various youth leagues in the Galicia area, was also now playing for Livingston, and we had chatted about the country and what I could expect. And the physical style of the football.

Like most people in Spain, I was aware that two massive clubs – Rangers and Celtic – dominated Scottish football. I had occasionally seen highlights of games involving both of those teams, and remembered watching the Champions League when Rangers played Valencia a couple of years before. They had impressed me with their level of quality and the standard of players in their team, even though they had lost out to a very good Valencia side with guys like Claudio Lopez and Gaizka Mendieta in their ranks.

In my mind I saw this trial at Raith as a huge opportunity for me; if I could win a contract – and then do well enough on the pitch – then maybe bigger clubs would come in for me.

I didn't set out with a target of trying to get a transfer to one of the Old Firm clubs, but I knew that with my speed and desire there could be the possibility of something bigger than Raith, with all due respect to them. And the guys I had talked to said that there were some big clubs outside of Rangers and Celtic that had excellent set-ups within the SPL, which had also attracted some very good foreign names to their squads.

The Raith manager, Peter Hetherston, had been impressed enough by what he'd seen of me in the videotapes that had been sent over. Now I had to make the most of the trial and convince the boss and the supporters that I could play.

The club arranged for us to stay in a B&B right next to their ground, Starks Park. When we pulled up in the car I got out and looked around – it was certainly a far cry from Ferrol! To be fair, despite the weather warnings I'd been given, it wasn't raining, although it was still pretty cold on what was supposed to be a summer's day.

I had a good attitude about what lay in front of me. I knew Kirkcaldy would be a millions miles away from Ferrol. I knew the stadium wouldn't be the Bernabeau! I knew this was a completely different world to the one that I had been raised in. But there was something about all these factors that I liked. It was a challenge. I was twenty-two years old, could not speak a word of English, and here I was pitching up at a club whose name I could barely even pronounce.

A lovely family ran the B&B and they made us very welcome. The first morning before we joined up with Raith for the start of our trial, Jorge and myself went down to the breakfast room and there was this hulk of a black guy sitting in the corner with his back to us. He was enormous and was munching his way through everything that was laid in front of him. As he turned round Jorge and I both looked at the battle-scars on his forehead and his rugged face – and quickly turned away. In Spanish, I said to Jorge: 'Look at the size of this guy. He looks like he could crush you with his bare hands!'

He was humming and singing away, then laughing and joking with the owners, all the time flashing this great big grin. As he got up to leave, he came over, shook both our hands and boomed: 'All the best boys,' before he charged out the door.

We sat there gazing at this guy. I know I am small, but I swear he was the biggest man I've ever seen.

It was Marvin Andrews. He still stayed in Kirkcaldy, even though he had moved from Raith Rovers to Livingston, as the town was home to the Zion Church he worshipped and preached at every day with his friend Pastor Joe. 'Big Marv' as everyone called him was to become a good friend and someone I would spend a lot of good times with later when our paths crossed again.

Jorge and myself headed off to meet our new teammates. From the minute I walked into the dressing room at Raith I felt at home. I liked the gaffer right away. He had a good way with the players and you could tell he was well respected. Peter was hard, but always fair. His number two was Kenny Black, again another good football man who clearly knew the coaching side of the game. Jorge spoke decent English, and did most of the translating for me when the gaffer wanted to pass things on, or when any of the other boys wanted to tell me something. Inside a day the only things I could say were 'Hello, my name is Nacho' and 'F—— off'. Well, that is the standard phrase required for a dressing room when the jokers start!

And there were plenty of characters at Raith. I met the chairman, Danny Smith, who I felt instantly was a decent man. They were all very friendly towards me. And honest and straight. They wanted me to sign, but I had to prove that what they had seen in the videos was for real.

The captain, big Shaun Dennis, was a great lad. Even though the club had not been used to foreigners in the past, there were no issues. We were included in everything. If there was a night out, Shaun would make sure we were invited. We tried not to be a Spanish clique – Jorge, Alvaro and myself – and I made every effort to very quickly integrate into the new surroundings that I found myself in.

I liked the town of Kirkcaldy, and the people. To be honest, I sleep quite a lot and still do after training when I go home. I would get back to the B&B in the afternoons and crash out. Then, later on, I would go for a walk around the shops. Despite the fact no one could understand a word I was saying, they were always very friendly. It's a good town, with honest types, and I liked that. If I was out myself I would end up doing sign language or drawing pictures of the things I wanted in the supermarket that I couldn't find. You could see these people staring at me thinking, 'Who the hell is this wee guy?'

The club were keen to get me signed up on a contract a few days into the trial. Jorge was also offered a deal which pleased me as we had become good friends and I relied on him to help me with the language barriers. To have a companion from your own country at a club is always an added bonus.

I held talks with the manager and the chairman and my agent agreed a two-year contract. My salary was around £1700 a month and the club also paid for my accommodation costs.

Back home in Ferrol things had started to settle down a bit, which eased my worries about leaving. Mum was getting stronger after the break-up of her marriage. Arantxa was doing really well at basketball, following in mum's footsteps after her handball career. So I had no hesitation in signing for Raith. Everything about the move just felt right and I was excited about playing in a new environment. With the blessings of the two women in my life, Kirkcaldy was to be my new home.

Quite quickly, myself, Jorge and Alvaro moved into a new flat in the town. They would look after me, cooking paella's and other Spanish dishes to remind us of home.

The club were excellent with me in terms of setting up bank accounts for my wages and helping me out with anything at all that I needed.

Training at Raith was good. It was a decent standard. The boys didn't hold back, which was good for me as I knew that it would be rough and tumble when the action started for real in the First Division.

On 4 August 2001 I made my Raith Rovers debut. I scored in a 2-2 draw at Airdrie, which got me off to a good start with our fans who had travelled through to the game. Three days later, in the Challenge Cup, I scored a double away at East Fife as we won 3-2. Three goals in the first two games; I could not have asked for a better start at my new club.

Containing my temper has always been an issue with me, both on and off the field. It can be a difficult thing to curb if it's in your nature and there have been many times when I've looked back on things and wished that I had been able to stop the red-mist from descending. Unfortunately, on my home debut against Partick Thistle, I again let my temper get the better of me. I was sent off for two bookings as we lost the game 2-1. I was gutted. The gaffer had a word and told me these things happen. But I felt like I had let Peter and my teammates down. It had been a good start for me. I was playing well, but I should have stayed out of trouble.

After serving a one-game suspension, I returned to the team. And the goal trail. Back to back doubles against Falkirk, in the League Cup, and Arbroath in the league, took my tally for the season so far to seven in six games. The fans were beginning to take to me.

When I went out and about in the town they would come up and shake my hand or ask for an autograph. I was getting good reports in the press with some people already saying my goals could help Raith win the title and promotion!

We had made a decent start to the campaign and I was settling in every day. Sure, I missed home. But the other Spanish boys helped me along and I talked a lot with my mum and sister on the phone to check everything was OK.

I also started to get a feel for Scotland. I would go through to Edinburgh to look around the shops or to see some of the sights. All the initial concerns that I had about moving away from Spain were quickly disappearing and I liked the way the people – no matter where I went – always made you feel welcome.

On the pitch I wasn't getting the same treatment. The First Division is a tough league. There were a lot of good sides like St Mirren, Hamilton Accies, Partick Thistle, Falkirk and Inverness all battling to get up with the big boys. That made every point a prisoner. And there were no prisoners taken on the pitch either! I had to take a few challenges that were, to say the least, tough. Even my speed wasn't enough sometimes to get me away from late tackles and I did find it hard not to react right away. Or store it in my mind and then have a go later. This, of course, got me into more trouble with the referees and I picked up a lot of bookings.

After a decent start to the season, victories had started to be very hard to come by and we began to slide down the table. I had been contributing well with goals, scoring twice as we beat St Mirren 3-0 at home and once in a 2-0 away win at Falkirk in the cup, which proved we could more than match the best. The team was not mirroring my own personal form – and just four months into my time at Raith an interesting proposal from England came my way.

Jorge Leira, who worked for my agency in Madrid, had now taken over my affairs. It had been arranged, through some of his contacts, for me to go for a week's trial at Norwich City. Raith gave their permission for me to travel down.

To be honest, things just never got off the ground down there. I was happy to go and have a look around, and to see what the manager, Nigel Worthington, thought about signing me. I knew nothing at all about the club, but it was worth taking a look. The problem for me was that it was just a five-day training stint, with no games. In my opinion it's very hard to judge a player correctly only from training sessions.

I went there every day, trained with the other players who were nice enough, and then just went back to the hotel. To be honest I didn't get much of a feel for the place, or for the manager, who didn't say much.

We basically agreed that he would stay in touch with Jorge and that was it. Off I went after five days in Norwich, back to Kirkcaldy. I wasn't too disappointed when it appeared nothing more would come of it. But I was pleased that a club had taken notice of me. Hopefully, I thought, that would be a sign of things to come.

With the Norwich experience quickly out of my mind, I began to again focus on life back at Raith, with our season starting to descend quickly into a relegation battle after such a promising start.

The gaffer was under pressure due to the results. It was hard to see that happening to him as I have always been someone who feels a responsibility to the manager. He sends the team out and it's up to the players to do the business – but it's always a manager who pays the price as he is easier to sack than an entire squad.

I had seen a hard side to Peter. In a game against Arbroath, just as the heat was really being turned up on him, he had gone crazy at me for an incident that was pretty embarrassing. I was caught late in a tackle by a defender and, again, reacted badly. As I ran by the guy I spat at him, which is a disgusting act and something I am pretty ashamed of looking back, and the fact it missed him didn't make the crime any less.

As any player will say, you would rather an opponent punched you or even put the head on you rather than being spat on.

I didn't think anyone had seen me spitting, and just got on with the game. But Peter had spotted what happened. I think he had kept his eye on the aftermath of the challenge in the knowledge that I had a tendency to react.

When we got into the dressing room after the game he went mental at me, shouting and swearing in my face and saying that spitting was not the way at his club, or indeed for any player in Scotland. I was left in no uncertain terms that he was disgusted with me. And he was right. I learned a lesson from Peter that day. Even though my reactions to things that sometimes happened on the pitch remained as volatile, there was no more spitting.

When we lost 3-1 at home to Ross County at the start of December the fans were calling for his head. I looked at Peter in the dressing room afterwards and, for the first time since I had signed for him back in July, I could see that he was losing heart. Three days after that defeat he resigned as manager.

I was really upset when he left, as he had been the guy who took a chance on me and gave me my break in Scotland. I had always given Peter everything I had on the pitch and I am sure he would admit that now. My record under him was fourteen goals in eighteen appearances, but that had not been enough to get us points in a lot of games and he felt it was better for him to leave.

The new manager was Jocky Scott. Most of the players at the club knew a lot about him and said he was an experienced manager with a good reputation in the game. When he arrived it was clear he was a different type of manager from Peter. More old school.

But he told the players we could still get out of the relegation danger we had now moved into. I didn't really get to know Jocky that well at all. In his first game in charge against Airdrie he dropped all of the foreign players. We sat in the stand and the team lost the game. This, by all accounts, did not amuse the chairman Danny Smith and we were all involved again against Hamilton Accies in the Scottish Cup. I came on as a sub, but we lost 1-0, leaving us a clear run at the league and still enough games to dig the club out of the hole.

As is often the case when a new manager takes over, there was a reaction in terms of the results. After a barren run I started to find my sights again in front of goal. I was determined to keep Raith up. There were plenty of rumours that I would be moving on regardless of what happened, and I was aware of interest in me from teams back in Spain, through my agent Jorge.

We won four of the next seven matches, also drawing one. I scored six goals over that run of results and I think the whole town believed we would be able to stave off the threat of dropping down to the Second Division.

Jocky's training was good. His motivation was also good, but the problem at Raith that season was consistency. By the beginning of March there were eight games left for us to stay alive, but we crashed and burned. Many fans I have talked to since say that the problem was that when I didn't score, no one else could step in.

The facts in the final eight games were that I managed to find the net just twice. And we only managed to win one game. So maybe the supporters' theory was right. I ended the season scoring twenty-two goals at a team that got relegated. Raith were down to the Second Division for the first time in fifteen years and that hit the town hard. It has always been one of my biggest regrets that the goals I scored didn't keep the team up, as Raith Rovers will always be special to me. But, in football, life always goes on. And for me the next stage in my Scottish adventure was about to unfold.

4

DUNDEE

I had plenty of options in the summer of 2002 after it became clear that my days at Raith Rovers were coming to an end. Jorge had informed me of a lot of interest from clubs back in Spain, and also in England, and although there were always times that I missed my own country, I was beginning to like the idea of continuing to play abroad.

It had been a good first year for me at Raith Rovers. I felt I had grown as a person as well as a player after sampling life in Scotland and the First Division and I had managed to pick up English to a decent standard as well. I liked Scotland, it felt like home.

Deep down I wanted to play in the SPL. I had watched a lot of games in the top division on TV and I was convinced that I could operate at that level. So when Dundee had a £100,000 offer accepted by Raith Rovers for me I was excited about fulfilling that dream.

They were a club on the up. There was a big Spanish speaking South American influence there and the manager, Ivano Bonetti, also had a good reputation. They were signing players from Venezuela and Georgia and I thought it looked like an interesting prospect to be a part of the revolution that was taking place.

There was also the prospect of matches against the Old Firm and derby games against Dundee United. I agreed a three-year contract, with Raith to get a fifteen per cent cut of any future transfer, which also pleased me. They were the club that had given me my break. If I did well, and was sold on, they would get a bit of extra money and I felt I owed them that.

My early conversations with Bonetti were good. I liked the way he talked about the game, his idea to play me right through the middle as a striker, and the fact it was a very decent squad meant Dundee were primed for a good season.

Players like Beto Carranza, Jonay Hernandez, Fabian Caballero, Julian Speroni, Brent Sancho, Juan Sara and Georgi Nemsadze were all in place and they had a lot of good Scottish players like Barry Smith, Lee Wilkie and Gavin Rae as well.

As a crazy chain of events turned out, I ended up falling somewhere between Bonetti's last signing and Jim Duffy's first. Bonetti left his position as manager before I could get there to start working with him. A lot of the discussions for my transfer had been through the Marr brothers, Jimmy and Peter, who owned the club, and they assured Jorge there would be no issues even though a new manager was coming in.

Duffy was appointed and it was a bit strange for me, as I had just been signed by the guy he had replaced, but we talked about the situation and I got a good feeling about Duffy right away. Again, you could tell he was a real football guy and he was excellent with the players from the very first day. It could not have been easy for him, walking into a club to take over a squad that was fairly cosmopolitan and had been pieced together by his successor, but he was honest and up front.

He told us what he expected from us, what we could expect from him and the standards he would set. There were no grey areas. I liked that. Nothing was hidden, and we all looked forward to working with him.

For me it was maybe different to some of the other guys who had been Bonetti signings and had to get used to a new boss with different methods. I never worked with Bonetti so it was just a complete fresh start under Duffy.

I quickly moved into a new house in Broughty Ferry, which is a lovely town just outside of Dundee. A lot of the players lived there, so it was a good community for me to be in.

Pre-season was going well under Duffy, although I did notice right away the step-up in standard from Raith Rovers.

As most clubs do, we headed abroad to fine-tune our preparations for the new campaign, to Romania, and after just a few days at the club I was embroiled in my first controversy. We should maybe have known that this would be a trip not without incident when, just a couple of days in, four of the boys were involved in a car crash in the streets of Bucharest!

Lee Wilkie, Gavin Rae, Steven Robb and Lee Mair were in a cab that collided with another taxi after the driver got lost and reversed down a one-way street. Whilst we had a bit of a laugh afterwards when we found out at the team hotel, both of the cars were badly damaged and it was just fortunate for the guys that none of them was injured.

On the pitch, things had started well. I scored in a draw against Rapid Bucharest, who were a good side, which was obviously a boost after just joining the club and only being a couple of weeks into my settling in period. Then I scored in the other game in the tournament against Electromagnetica.

But the next night I found myself embroiled in a bit of bother – with the Romanian mafia!

The organisers of the tournament had arranged a party at a casino, which the manager, the players, and the Dundee officials had to attend. Duffy said to us we could have a few beers and a night off, as we were getting ready to go home after a hard training stint. I was never a massive drinker. I had a few beers and was merry, but not ridiculously drunk. The lads were having a good night and there was not a hint of trouble.

The casino was over three levels and I started making my way up the stairs to the top level where the manager and most of the other guys were. As I got to the top of the first set of stairs this guy was in front of me and wouldn't move.

I tried to get around him, but he kept blocking me. I said to him, in Spanish, 'Why don't you get out of my f—— way?'

The guy muttered something back – in Spanish – and I was a bit shocked that he had understood what I had just said seeing as we were in the middle of Bucharest, but he obviously knew my language.

I got past him, eventually, and then went up the next flight of stairs. But he was following me all the way, shouting in Spanish that he wanted an apology. When we got to the top level, there were two bouncers on either side of the door going in to the private area that had been set aside for the team. I could see the gaffer, some of the other players and officials, all inside.

But this guy would not leave it. He was shouting and pointing, and by this stage there was a bit of a scene. Duffy and some of the other players came out and got involved.

When I say involved, it was the usual situation where people get in the middle and keep the two people who have the issue apart. Duffy was telling me to relax and just leave it, and I was happy to do that, but this guy was going crazy and I was beginning to feel the red mist descend. I was being held around my arms from behind by one of the Dundee boys, and he was being held as well.

Then, in a flash, the smaller of the two bouncers – this guy was not as tall as me but he was built like an ox – just popped out of the mass of bodies and punched me right in the face. He caught me bang on the nose and the blood just starting pouring. After that, I just lost it. Duffy told the other players to get me out as quickly as possible, and Jonay Hernandez more or less grappled me down the stairs and out into the street whilst people from the club tried to sort out the mess upstairs.

We waited on a taxi and Jonay was still holding on to me. I said: 'I'm fine, just let me go.' I think Jonay knew what was coming, but he let go of me anyway. In a second, I just darted away and tried to get back into the casino. In my mind, this bouncer had taken a liberty by punching me when my hands were trapped behind my back and I wanted revenge.

It must have been funny to onlookers watching as my team-mates – bearing in mind I'd only been at the club a couple of weeks – all chased me to stop me from going back in. A few minutes later, Duffy came down and told Jonay to make sure I got into a car and got back to my room. We made the short ride back and I was swearing and shouting all the way, covered in blood.

Back in the room, I tried to clean myself up a bit. Any effects of the drink had worn off now, but I was livid. I started to take it out on the hotel room, throwing things around and Jonay was ducking for cover. He said to me: 'Nacho, you are f—— crazy. Calm down or the boss will go mad.' Eventually, I started to realise that there was no point carrying things on. I pulled myself together and got some ice for my face and nose.

I was sitting an hour later when there was a loud bang on the door. I opened it, and there in the corridor was Duffy with a big smile on his face.

He came in, asked me if I was alright and said just to forget it. As he was leaving, he turned and said: 'Lucky you got out of there wee man. Twenty minutes later two big people carriers turned up with a dozen or so huge bastards in black suits. I think you went to town with a guy from the Bucharest mafia!'

I shook my head and offered a nervous laugh. Maybe getting thrown into that taxi by Jonay had been the biggest bonus of the night!

With a good pre-season behind us, it was time to begin life in the SPL. I had a feeling early on that Duffy would play me more as a wide player, or that I would have to fight very hard to earn a place in the team. We had a lot of excellent strikers who had bigger reputations than me, but the challenge to establish myself as a regular first-team player was one I welcomed. I had settled in well at the club. The staff were great, and out and about in the town the fans were great. Well, the Dundee ones anyway.

The rivalry between Dundee and Dundee United was something I had obviously never experienced. It is probably viewed as the third biggest derby in the country behind Rangers and Celtic and Hearts and Hibs. Trust me, though, to the people of Dundee it means everything. The 2002/03 fixture list had thrown up a meeting just four games into the new season and from more or less the first kick of the ball in that campaign the fans were telling us how we had to beat United.

Every day I turned up at Dens – and looked the short distance up the road to Tannadice – it made me smile. It would be unheard of anywhere else for two teams to have a stadium each just a few hundred yards away on the same street. I thought it was a joke at first when I was told about it, but when I arrived in Dundee for the first time, there it was. Two stadiums, two clubs and one very, very big rivalry.

I got the impression that the United fans were a bit jealous of what was happening at Dens. A lot of money was being spent on foreign players, decent names, and I think they were concerned that they would lose their reputation of being the bigger club. Of course, the Dundee fans loved it. They were a passionate bunch of supporters, and I tried to forge a bond with them right away in the same way I had with the Raith fans.

My approach to the game, my effort every time I played, had to be absolute commitment to the cause. I wanted them to see right away I was worthy of a place in the team and that I would have my heart on my sleeve.

After starting the season with a 1-1 draw at home to Hearts, we travelled to Ibrox. It was my first look at the stadium and it was a wonderful arena. I had watched with interest what had been happening at Rangers. They had brought in Alex McLeish to replace Dick Advocaat and he had taken them to a couple of trophies already. They had some top players, far better than the results in the league the previous season had shown when Celtic had again been champions, so it was always going to be a daunting task for us going to Glasgow, even with the confidence of a point in the bag from our opener against Hearts.

I got the nod to start again from Duffy, which was a huge confidence boost in front of almost 50,000 fans, the biggest crowd I had ever played in front of.

Rangers had the likes of Lorenzo Amoruso, Arthur Numan, Barry Ferguson, Mikel Arteta, Ronald De Boer, Shota Arveladze and Tore Andre Flo in their side. That was a reflection of the difference in quality. For the first time I had seen close up the power of the Old Firm.

I felt we had very good players at Dundee. We had guys with a lot of technical ability and class, but when De Boer scored early on, Rangers just moved through the gears. They ran out 3-0 winners and I sat in the dressing room at Ibrox afterwards thinking to myself, 'This is just another level.'

We knew we were never going to be able to compete with the Old Firm over the course and distance of a season. We had our own agenda to pursue, maybe looking to finish in the top six or do well in one of the cup competitions, and we also had the first derby of the season looming.

After our Ibrox experience, I was unfortunately to stumble back into dangerous territory with referees. We travelled to East End Park to play Dunfermline and although I had put us ahead twice in the game, making it 1-0 and 2-1, we lost two goals late on that took them 4-2 ahead. I had already been booked, but the red mist came down again. It was something I had tried really hard to drum into my mind; that I had to keep control as the bookings and red cards at Raith had cost me games when I was left sitting in the stand through suspension.

I knew that, with the squad Dundee had, dropping out of the team would make it very tough to win a place back, but I picked up another yellow card from the ref for a stupid foul and was sent packing. Duffy wasn't best pleased, but he didn't have to tell me, I knew I had to sort that side of things out or I would simply not be picked as it was hard enough to get results in a tough SPL, never mind going down to ten men.

After serving my one game ban, I returned for the first derby of the season at Tannadice. It was an amazing experience. When you went to get the ball for a throw-in or take a corner, there were all sorts of things being shouted by the United fans. Maybe for the best, I didn't quite understand all of what they were saying!

It was a typical derby game; tackles flying in and plenty of niggle and aggro between the players. I loved it. And, naturally, I did get my customary booking. The game ended in a hard fought draw, which is no good for either set of fans who crave wins in these games, but always better than losing.

It had been a decent start from us and I was happy with my own form, having scored three goals and started all the matches I was available for. However, things started to come off the rails a bit.

As many people have observed about me throughout my career, I am a 'confidence' player. I can go on runs and get a lot of goals, but when things are not going well I tend to let my head drop too much and it can have a negative effect.

I was taken to Dundee to score goals, but they started to dry up. It became so bad that I went nine matches without a goal and that led to Duffy leaving me on the bench three or four times over that period. I totally understood that, although in my defence, I was being played more in the wide area, which is neither my best, nor my natural position.

We were having up and down results, the performances not as consistent as they should have been. I think that, even though Dundee were fairly new to the SPL, the target of the Marr brothers had been a top six finish given the level of investment.

Duffy chopped and changed things around and I did manage to find the net against Hibs and Livingston, but I just never seemed to get going with the kind of form I wanted. After the goal against Livingston, which came at the end of November, I once more went on another nine-game barren run. In contrast to my own scoring exploits, the team were beginning to get going. We picked up more points, even getting draws in some games that we were losing earlier in the season, and there was the morale boosting 3-2 win over United in the return derby fixture to keep our fans happy.

By the time we went to Tannadice again, in early February, we had already taken care of Partick Thistle away in the Scottish Cup. Duffy started me in the derby. I think he new that I was the kind of player who thrived on the passion of these occasions, even more so at Tannadice when we were the away team and the underdogs.

We had a dreadful start when Dave Mackay scored an own goal midway through the first period but I finally found my shooting boots to equalise and we headed back across the road with a 1-1 draw. I always found it mad; we walked home to Dens to get our cars from games at Tannadice. Where else in the world would a team be able to walk back from a match!

A couple of weeks later we had another big match, this time at home to Aberdeen in the Scottish Cup. That was always another match that gave the fans an edge, as they were a team with a big reputation and there had been some major matches down through the years between the clubs.

With one of our best performances of the season, and with me again on the score-sheet, we beat them 2-0 to make it through to the last eight. We were certainly hitting the gas in terms of our performances and results at the business end of the campaign, and winning the cup was beginning to be mentioned.

A surge up the SPL took us into the top six, which was a fantastic achievement. And, despite needing a replay after I scored in a 1-1 draw at Brockville, we battered Falkirk 4-1 at Dens Park to make it through to the semis.

Duffy was doing a great job. He had the team playing really well for each other, and he knew the differing approaches with certain players. He knew I was a player who needed lifted from time to time, whereas others maybe needed a kick up the backside.

After a first half of the season in which we had struggled to find genuine consistency, we were going into the last few weeks of the campaign with a cup semi-final at Hampden against Inverness to look forward to, and five matches against the other top six sides, including the Old Firm who were fighting it out for one of the tightest championships in years.

Unfortunately, I was back on another barren run. Duffy benched me again, which was a disappointment, even though I came on as a sub at Hampden when we beat Caley 1-0 to make it through to the Scottish Cup Final.

I also started at Parkhead in a real night to forget. The title was coming down to goal difference, possibly, and every time either Rangers or Celtic played they were trying to score as many as they could.

We were blown away 6-2 at Parkhead on a night when Celtic could have scored double that amount. It was a real thrashing, but the manager had made some changes to the team to try and keep everyone fresh with the final just a couple of weeks away.

Our opponents were to be Rangers. Of course, like everyone else in the country, the boys at Dundee were engrossed in the title race. I wanted Rangers to win it. I was quite clear on that to some of the lads in the Dundee dressing room who were Celtic fans.

Arteta was Spanish, and I had spoken to him a few times. I wanted to see my fellow Spaniard win the league, but we also knew that if Rangers had lost the league it might have seen them come into the final six days later on a real downer. We had guaranteed a place in Europe because Rangers were in the final and would be going into the Champions League qualification matches, but we wanted to win the cup on our own merits and get the Euro spot that way.

I came off the pitch after we went down 1-0 to Hearts to find out Rangers had won the title with more or less the last kick of the season. And it had been a penalty from Arteta. I was pleased for him but I wanted to beat them the next week and take the cup back to Dundee.

The build-up to the final was an amazing week. The whole club was buzzing with excitement as each day passed in the lead-up to Hampden. We had the media day, the official picture and the measuring up of the suits for the Final. It was great to be involved in such a huge event for Dundee. Of course, the nagging doubt for every player is wondering if you will play.

We felt we had a real chance of winning that Final. The Rangers players were emotionally and physically drained after the title had gone to the last seconds and there was a fair chance they would have spent the first couple of days of the week prior to the final still partying!

It was amazing when we got to Hampden. There were about 20,000 Dundee fans in the city and Duffy said to us, 'Win it for them, and win it for yourself.' I was gutted, though, when he named the team and I was a sub.

From the first whistle you could see Rangers were lethargic. It was a very warm day and they looked to have little in the legs. We played really well and probably should have made better use of the chances we did get. Then, as so often happens against one half of the Old Firm, Lorenzo Amoruso headed the opening goal from a corner. It was out of nothing, but Rangers had the lead.

Duffy put me on, almost right away. I was determined to make an impact. I felt, if we had scored and taken Rangers to extra-time, we might have won it, purely because we had more in the tank. But I missed a really good chance to get that equalising goal and the final just drifted away.

I sat slumped on the turf, watching the Rangers boys celebrate. It was the last game for Amoruso and Numan, both great players, and the Rangers fans were amazing. I thought to myself, 'God, both these boys will miss this.'

For Dundee, it was all about regrets. You wonder when one of the smaller clubs is going to get another crack at winning something.

My first season in the SPL had ended in real disappointment, and even though we had plaudits, we had reached the final and also made the top six with a UEFA Cup place to come the next season, it was a hard day from which to find any kind of satisfaction. That is just me. I always want to win.

I had started thirty matches and scored nine goals, which wasn't too bad, but I knew I had to step it up a gear, that I would only be allowed one season to bed in. That was my main aim as I headed back to Spain to see mum and Arantxa.

Dundee had become used to occupying the headlines outside of the Old Firm. I had read before I joined the club about an interest in them from a guy called Giovanni Di Stefano, who was an Italian lawyer. He had made the press due to links with the Serbian warlord, Arkan, which had caused a fair bit of a storm.

Not long after we returned for pre-season for the new 2003/04 campaign, he was again being linked with a role at Dens Park. It was just another chapter in what was fast becoming a mad story on Tayside.

People have often asked me since if, as players, we had any idea that trouble might have been going on behind the scenes financially. We had no idea, much like many years later at Rangers when money problems began to bite. As a player, you go in every day, train, play the games and conduct yourself in a professional manner. You never get involved in what's going on in the boardroom, just like you would never want any directors getting involved in the dressing room.

I have no doubt people were looking at Dundee and asking, 'How can they afford this?' But it was never an issue for us, as long as we were getting paid and doing our jobs. A couple of years before, the club had made its biggest ever signing when Claudio Caniggia was brought to Dundee. He was one of the biggest names in the game, even though he had been in and out of the business after his well-documented drug problems. He shone at Dundee and was taken to Rangers by Dick Advocaat.

If the Dundee fans thought that Caniggia was as big as it was going to get, then another huge name lay around the corner – and Di Stefano played his part. He was made a director of the club in early August and was quickly in the press talking about more and more major plans and claims that big names would be coming in.

Duffy had to keep the dressing room focused. We had to hit the ground running in the SPL and prepare for UEFA Cup qualification matches, which were a reward for reaching the cup final the year before.

After an outstanding 3-0 win at Motherwell on the opening day, we faced Spartak Trnava in the first round. I scored my first European goal as we won the first leg 2-0. To have scored in the UEFA Cup was a huge confidence boost and I followed that up with a double at home to Livingston in a 2-1 SPL win before another two goals helped see off the Albanian's courtesy of a second leg 4-0 thrashing.

By the time we brought the curtain down on August – with a 1-1 draw at Kilmarnock with me on the score-sheet again – I had scored six times in six games and was really flying. And so were the club. A week later Craig Burley, the former Celtic and Scotland midfielder, was unveiled as our latest signing. And the week after that another world-class name rolled in – Fabrizio Ravanelli.

I was a bit awe struck when he arrived. This guy had been a striker of the highest calibre in his time with Juventus and Italy – and here he was in the same dressing room. Rava was a really cool guy. He mixed in right away and was by no means full of himself.

He was still a top finisher, as I saw in training every day, even if he had slowed up a bit. It was a joy to be training alongside him every day and I was determined to learn as much as I could. With these two experienced additions, I felt we were set for another very good season.

Unfortunately, we landed as tough a draw as we could have in the UEFA Cup, against the Italian side Perugia. We lost the first leg at Dens 2-1, which left a huge mountain to climb going to their place as, traditionally, Italian sides always get the job done. They beat us 1-0 and the Euro dream was over. But on a personal note, the goals just kept flying in.

I scored against Rangers, Hearts, Partick Thistle, a penalty in the 1-1 derby draw with United and also Hibs. By the start of November I had found the net thirteen times and was in the form of my career so far. Duffy was delighted with me. I told him that, when I got on a run, I was a real confidence player. Unfortunately, just as things started to look really good for the club, a disaster was to strike. As I have said, finances were never an issue for the players, but we arrived at training one morning in early November to discover that Dundee was in serious trouble.

The spending had obviously caught up and the club were being threatened with administration. It was a nightmare. Of course, the first thought you have is for yourself. I had no idea what would happen in terms of the contracts we had signed, if we would be sold, if we would even be paid if we stayed, or if the club itself would survive. But there was also the tears on the faces of all the staff at the club, in the offices and the kitchen, the ground staff. It was a horrible, horrible time, waiting and wondering what the future would hold.

The press, naturally, were all over it. Dundee had been something of a fairytale over the previous couple of years, getting into the SPL, signing all these foreigners and spending big money. Now it had all come crashing down.

Fifteen players were to be released by the administrators – including Burley, Ravanelli and Fabian Caballero – which had a crushing effect on morale. These were guys who were team-mates and it was dreadful to see them being cast aside, but it was the only way the club could survive and that was the main aim. I was lucky in the fact I had been doing well, had a long-term contract and maybe they looked at me and felt there would be some kind of transfer market value.

We played Dunfermline on the Saturday and lost 2-0, which was no real surprise given what was going on. We were informed that the club, on the Monday, would officially be in the hands of the administrators and the cuts would come into play right away.

It was agreed between some of the boys that we should go out for a night in Dundee, to have a few beers and try to boost morale a bit given what was going on at the club. A whole crowd of us went to a few bars, then other players joined us late on, and we headed to that well know Dundee hot spot, Fat Sams.

We had a decent enough night, and then headed out to get a taxi. I was with Brent Sancho, Stephen McNally and Jonay Hernandez.

Big Brent – who was as nice a guy as you could ever meet but built like an absolute ox – and I were a bit ahead and we walked past a couple of big lads, who were clearly the worse for wear. Brent said to me, 'Let's walk up a bit wee man,' as we both sensed there could be a bit of trouble.

A taxi quickly appeared and big Brent jumped in the front, with me getting in the back. As he tried to shut the door, one of the guys we had just passed by blocked it and said: 'This is our taxi, you black bastard,' and proceeded to haul Brent out of the front seat.

I had a few drinks in me, to be fair, but I was shocked. It was a dreadful thing to hear anyone say such a racist remark, as it as not anything I had come across in Scotland before. Brent did not take kindly to what he had just been called and a real fracas developed with all sorts of grappling and shoving going on. We were all in the middle of it with this moron and his pal.

The police arrived and Brent, Stephen and myself were all arrested and taken to the cells of the police station in Dundee. We were charged with assault the next day, which was the last thing the club needed in terms of PR given that we had just gone into financial meltdown.

Duffy was not happy. We were called in to explain what had happened and we gave our side of events. I defy anyone to say that they would not have reacted had they been out with a friend who had been subjected to racist abuse in that way. It was sickening and I would react with the same anger tomorrow if a similar incident occurred. I was later cleared of the charges and never stood trial and both Brent and Stephen were also found not guilty a year later, which was the correct outcome.

There was so much going on at the club that we maybe didn't get dealt with as harshly as we would have done had it been a stable ship. It was, obviously, a regrettable incident, as you don't want to be getting into trouble with the police. But racist comments kicked it all off and that could not be forgotten. None of us were looking for trouble, just to get home after a night out.

I tried to focus on my game again but the impact of the administration had a huge bearing on the team and our numbers.

Results began to slide and I felt really sorry for the fans, and for Duffy. The supporters had been riding the crest of a wave and then it was suddenly down to earth with a bump. And the manager? He had built a squad for the season, only to see it slashed because of financial problems. We never really recovered from that dark time. By the time the January transfer window opened in 2004, there was huge speculation that Dundee would sell players to try and raise money. My name was mentioned a lot with clubs in England, teams back in Spain – and Rangers. I spoke with my mother about Rangers. She said: 'I think you'll sign for them one day, son.'

I asked her why she thought that. 'I like the name, I think it would suit you to play for them.' I had eighteen months left on my contract and by the start of January I had scored fifteen goals, which was a good tally for a player outside of the Old Firm.

I resigned myself to the fact that I would be leaving Dundee. If it was to be in January, then fine – as long as the deal was right for me. If it was to be the summer, when we had a feeling more players would be shipped out, then I would wait and see what the options were. I was in a good enough position, I felt. I was making a good name for myself and I would not be rushed or pushed into anything that I didn't want to do. I banged in another three goals during the January window, which only intensified the speculation, but there was nothing concrete coming back from my agent, Jorge.

I told him: 'Speak to me when we have something hard and fast.' That was always my understanding with him as I wanted to focus totally on my game. If I was to leave Dundee, the more goals I scored, the better the player I became, which might increase the number of teams interested in signing me.

Just days after the window slammed closed – with me still at Dens – we had the chance to book another spot at Hampden, this time in the League Cup. Having dealt with Clyde and Hearts in the earlier rounds, we faced Livingston at the neutral venue of Easter Road.

They had a decent side and, with the way we had been weakened, we were no longer viewed as favourites to get through. Livi knocked us out with a last minute penalty and the bus journey back from Edinburgh to Dundee was a nightmare. I sat there thinking that, in a few short months, the team had fallen apart. We had been flying, the place was buzzing – and then it was over. It was a very negative situation. I knew it would be better for me to leave and the summer would be my time to get out.

But, just as I tried to get my head up for what would be a crucial run-in to the season if I wanted to attract more interest, my own world was to fall apart.

5

DEVASTATION

Like any son, I missed my mother. Life in Dundee was good, I was settled in Scotland and I had met a lot of new friends. Where I was as a person, my confidence, my contentment at the start of 2004 was a million miles away from the small Spanish kid who had stepped off the plane in Edinburgh a couple of years before to begin life outside my own country, without my family, without a word of English.

But I missed my mum. I missed Arantxa. I had agreed with mum that she would come over to Scotland and stay with me as soon as she had Christmas out of the way and tied up whatever she had to take care of back in Ferrol that would allow her to have a decent break with me. This was a big thing for her as well, as she would have to leave Arantxa, but my mum knew how much it would mean having her over with me for a decent length of time.

She arrived, finally, at the end of January. As you would expect, she was going around inspecting my place in Broughty Ferry, trying to take over right away. Just being a normal mum. We did a bit of sightseeing, going to the shops in Edinburgh, which pleased her, and we just hung out together. I kind of got the feeling that was all mum wanted to do, just spend some time with me.

For the past few years I had been away, due to my career, living in Huesca, then Kirkcaldy and Dundee, and it was hard for her as we had been so close in Spain. That suited me, as I loved my mum with all my heart. Just having her over to see me play in a couple of games, even sitting watching TV or coming in from training or a game to a nice paella was great. It felt like the old days when she would listen to me moaning about this and that to do with football. She would say, 'Nacho – never give up, always keep going and you will succeed.' It took a lot to knock my mother over now. She had been in some very dark places, gone through hell really, but she was back to the strong, loving mother I had always known.

It was her bond with her kids that led her to put me on the spot one day when I came in from training. She had been with me for a fortnight, but I could tell she was also missing Arantxa.

'I think I'll go back and see your sister for a week,' mum said to me. 'Then I'll come back here for another couple of weeks. I miss her, Nacho, and I can see you are fine.' She gave me a big hug. I knew mum had seen what she wanted to see. I was OK; she could go check on the other one now. And then she would be back. We were her life. All that mattered.

Of course, I knew where she was coming from. My sister was still young and needed mum as well. I was never going to be selfish. We got the flights booked for her to go back to Ferrol and I took her the next day to the airport in Edinburgh.

As we walked through to the departure gates she was smiling. She told me, as she always did, how proud she was of me and that she would be back in a week. I hugged her, gave her a kiss on the cheek and waved goodbye, reminding her to call me from London as she waited for the connection to Madrid, and then on to La Coruna which was the nearest airport to our house.

A couple of days later, I took the phone call that was to change my world forever. We had been given a couple of days off by the club at the start of the week and Jonay Hernandez and myself had headed over to Amsterdam for a short break. As we were preparing to come back from Holland, my sister rang, in a complete state.

My mum had been rushed to hospital in Ferrol after taking unwell. Tests quickly showed there was a problem with an artery in her heart and she would require an emergency operation. I was frantic and initially looked at heading to Spain straight from Holland.

But the situation in Spain moved pretty quickly. Mum was operated on, and by the time I had flown back to Edinburgh, Arantxa gave me the positive news that she was OK. She had come through things and the doctors were happy.

We had a game against Dunfermline on the Saturday, but the manager told me I was to head back home right away if that's what I wanted to do. My mum's family – she had three sisters and one brother – were all keeping me informed of what was happening along with my sister. Mum was stable. I thanked God.

I spoke again with the manager. He said the decision was up to me, but I had been reassured by my family that she was OK. I played against Dunfermline and then headed on a flight from Edinburgh down to London. It was the last flight on the Saturday night so I slept overnight in Heathrow as I wanted to be on the first plane to Madrid in the morning.

I was speaking a lot with my uncle Ricardo, and my aunt Maruja and they were more or less giving me an hour-by-hour account of what was happening. Arantxa was only nine-teen years old, still very young, and she was very, very upset. I knew I had to get there, I wanted to see mum. But my family had said she was doing well so just to stay calm and get there as quickly as I could.

Sometime between my flights from Heathrow to Madrid, my mum passed away. There had been a major complication, a clot in the artery, and a second operation had failed to save her. When I landed in Madrid, she had already gone. When I phoned my uncle Ricardo to say I was waiting on the short flight to Coruna, I sensed a change in his voice. He didn't want to tell me, as they knew I was flying alone. When I finally reached home, I learned the news. My mum had died at the age of forty-three. I collapsed to my knees and shut my eyes.

It was the first time in my life that I had that kind of feeling and I don't ever wish to have it again. I could simply not take in what had happened. Less than a week before, we had been joking and laughing as I walked her to the departure gate at Edinburgh Airport.

It was simply unbelievable. My entire family was there, and everyone just kept looking at Arantxa and myself. She was nineteen and I was twenty-four. Our mother had been taken from us. Our father was no longer part of our lives. Everyone who looked at us just cried and cried. I sat there staring at them, staring at my sister, one part of me trying to understand how God could have let this happen, how my mum could have been taken from us. Then the other thoughts started to creep in. What would this mean for me? How could I go back to Scotland and leave my teenage sister by herself? It was total and utter devastation, uncertainty, anger and pain – everything all rolled into one.

Over the following few days we had to arrange the funeral and speak to a lot of friends and family who were asking how my sister and I were. We were lucky to have such a loving family unit behind us. My dad also phoned and I spoke with him for the first time in years. It was a strange call as my mother's passing had put us back in contact, but it sometimes takes these tragedies for people to speak. I was civil to him, as my mind was still racing and my heart was still broken. There was more going on that needed looked after rather than having any kind of issues with him.

The club were excellent in the support they offered me. I got a lot of phone calls from the manager and my teammates all saying to let them know if there was anything they could do. That meant a lot, to know that Dundee was rallying around me as well. Duffy told me to take as long as I needed. He knew I was crushed and football had slipped way into the background.

The funeral, as any child will tell you when they have to bury a parent, was the worst day of my life. It had been difficult in the build up as just going around the house – without mum being there – had been strange. I felt it very uncomfortable, even though it was my own home. In truth, I just didn't know what to do.

The day came and went when we had to say goodbye to mum and, as is often the case, you find strength from within to get through it. It was strange listening to the service and then talking to people afterwards. They spoke about mum in such glowing terms, what a great mother she had been. But, even then, I still found it hard to comprehend. It was as though they were talking about someone else. Not my mum. I still believed she would walk through the door.

I knew I had to address things right away with Arantxa.

She was my responsibility now but, even though she was growing into a beautiful woman in her own right and pursuing her own sporting career as a fine basketball player, I knew she was still a kid.

I sat her down. I said to Arantxa: 'I will leave Dundee right away, terminate my contract and get a job back here in Spain. I don't want to play football anymore. It's just not the same, now that mum has gone.'

I was being absolutely genuine. In my mind I felt the right thing to do was to quit my career and go home to Spain. Arantxa was shocked, and even got a bit angry.

She shouted: 'Nacho, do you think mum would want that? You made her so proud, you made all of us so proud. She would NEVER want you to give up on your dreams. Go back – and be a great player for her. I will be fine.'

The tears were streaming down my face. Already, I could see my mum in her. Strong willed and determined. She told me that she would be doing everything she could to pursue her career in my mum's honour – and I had to do the same.

With that sorted out, I prepared to head back to Scotland. I didn't know if I could see through what Arantxa had asked me to do, as my heart was still shattered. But being in the house, every day, was beginning to kill me. I had to get out of there, try to move on a tiny bit at least. I had to go back to Dundee.

On my return, the love and warmth from the other players and the club really overwhelmed me. I think the guys knew I was a kind of deep person. They didn't want me to be sitting around by myself, so I would get dragged out for dinner to one of the boys' houses, or just to watch a European game on TV, anything to keep my mind off what had just happened, even though that was tough.

I spoke with the manager and told him that I wanted to play against Kilmarnock at Rugby Park on the Saturday. It had been two weeks since my last game against Dunfermline and I wanted to get back out on the pitch again and try to put all the pain and hurt to the back of my mind. He was happy with that.

Just six minutes into the match I managed to score and put Dundee a goal up. I pointed to the sky, as if to say, 'That was for you, mum.' It was the most emotional I have ever felt when scoring a goal. But I was pleased to have done it, to get back to playing. We lost the game 4-2, but for me it was about just playing again. Trying to take the first step back on the road.

Even with football once more able to occupy my thoughts, it was still very difficult to get over what had just happened. It had taken me a long time after moving away from Spain to feel assured that my mum and sister were OK back home. But at least they had each other. Now, as well as having to cope with my mother's death, my sister was having to handle being by herself, and she wasn't old enough for that. I had promised her that I would end all thoughts of quitting football, but there were several occasions when my mind did drift again back down that road.

The end to the season also didn't help me. The financial turmoil had taken its toll on Dundee. The year before we were top six and had a Scottish Cup Final on the horizon but this run in was all about the bottom six as we had gone on a fairly dramatic slide.

There is no doubt my form dipped. I just couldn't get my head right. I scored one goal in eight games, but my mind was a mess. What did the future hold? Where would I be, as it looked as though Dundee would sell me in the summer?

Did I even want to keep playing? Going out every week with these kinds of issues weighing me down was very tough.

I tried to kick on, but there was not much left in my legs. As the season petered out, I thought that, if it was going to be the end for me at Dens, then I would try to go out with some goals. I attempted to re-focus, all the while battling with the demons in my mind.

Thankfully, after all the support the club and the fans had given me, I scored in my final two games of the season, both at home. I found the net once in a 2-0 win over Kilmarnock and twice in a win by the same scoreline against Livingston. That pleased me. I had at least been able to give the club something back.

The speculation had mounted again about my situation, with Rangers being heavily linked alongside other teams, such as Fulham. There was a bit of interest noted with Jorge, but I had switched my mind off. I just wanted to get away from it all. As soon as the season ended, one of the most turbulent years of my life on and off the pitch, I just headed back to Spain and put everything to one side.

Dundee was in a mess. I knew, deep down, I would be transferred, but that was not a thought at the forefront of my mind. Going to Ferrol, trying to find some kind of solace and being there for Arantxa was all that mattered. I had finished the season with twenty-four goals from forty three appearances and given my all. What would be would be.

I have no problem being honest and admitting this – the death of my mother changed me forever. I have always been an emotional person, and more often than not I carried that into football. If I was on the end of a defeat, and I am the same to this day, then I would go home and mull it around and around in my mind. But after my mother died, everything became worse. I sank into some deep, deep depressions. I could not get my head around the fact that, less than a week after I had waved goodbye to her as she went to board a flight, she was dead. The whole thing has changed me. The people who are close to me, like my fiancée Donna and my family, wonder why I take things so badly. 'There are ten other players in the team,' they will say to me. I link it all back to my mum dying.

I know that people say time heals things. But others say that, in some cases, an individual can never truly get over losing someone close. I think that has been the case with me.

I have tried to get on with my life since my mum's death, and I have moved on. I have grown and tried not to take things as personally when Rangers lost a game. But to this day I can still go into major depressions and look as though the weight of the world is on my shoulders. I don't think that will ever leave me to a certain extent, as I am thirty now. OK, when I stop playing I might not have as many situations that put me into bad moods. Football can do that, if you care as much as me. I have looked at some players and, to be honest, they don't seem to take defeat the way I do. That is up to them, but when Rangers lost a game that I had played in I would be very, very down and start to question myself and all aspects of my performances.

Many players do that, but I think I go too far. As I have said, I put that all down to losing my mother. She is not there for a phone-call but she was the one who lifted me and got my head up. I don't know if people will understand it, but that's just the way I am. People will look at me and say, 'He's a footballer, he has nice things and gets well paid, he plays for Rangers – what has he got to worry about?'

But I am also a human being and a son who was left devastated at the age of twenty-five when my mum was taken in an instant. I hope to take steps forward and not have the same kind of depressions that I have had. And with the arrival of my son, Javier, who was born in January, I have a different focus now as well. I have become a parent for the first time and I have the same bond that my mum had with me. I aim to be the kind of parent to him that my mother was for me and my sister. But I have cried at the thought she never got to see him. She would have been a loving grandmother, and these are the cruel issues you have to try and get over.

Having to cope with my mother's sudden death did one thing, however. And that was bring my sister and I even closer together. We had always had an excellent relationship, but we knew we had to be there for each other at all times. And that has been the case since, even though Arantxa is getting on with her own life in Spain. She hasn't got married yet, and remains dedicated to her career as a professional basketball player in San Sebastian. I am so proud of the fact she represented Spain at the European Championships a few years ago. Unfortunately she has had to recover from two operations on her knees that have suffered due to playing on the hard courts. But she is a real fighter with tremendous spirit. We talk all the time on the phone and she comes over to stay with us in Glasgow as often as she can. I see a lot of my mother in her, especially her caring side. She is a proud aunt of Javier, and seeing her with him always makes me smile. So do the memories I have of my time with Arantxa and my mum as we grew up and battled through the tough times, the dark days.

I will never forget my mother. She made me the man I am today. Every day, I wish she were here.

6

HEARTACHE TO
HELICOPTER SUNDAY

The mentally exhausting battle to get to Rangers, and my decision to turn down Celtic, had really drained me over the summer of 2004. But I had left life in Dundee behind now and realised the dream. I knew all eyes would be on me as my signing saga had dragged on for so long. I had to prove that I could handle life at the club and that I had been worth the time, effort and money that Rangers had put into getting me. But I was not the only person at the club under major pressure – everyone around me was.

Rangers simply could not have finished the previous campaign in any worse state in terms of a title challenge. League tables never lie and, when the final curtain came down on 2003/04, a massive seventeen points separated the Old Firm.

I knew the Rangers fans would not accept that kind of gap. Missing out on the title to Celtic is bad enough. But getting beaten out of sight? Totally unacceptable.

I was surprised that Rangers had fallen apart so quickly the previous season. Sure, they had lost some big name stars from the treble season in 2002/03 and there was obviously not the same level of money for the manager to spend as in previous years. But they still had some top players and it should have been a lot closer. Having done so well the year before, it was a major disappointment to end the season with nothing.

It was down to the new players, myself included, to make sure we hit the ground running. There would be a Champions League qualifier early season, which was worth millions of pounds to the club. And there was no margin for error in the title battle.

Celtic were champions. They had a very strong squad and a manager, in the shape of Martin O'Neill, who had done little wrong. When I had come up against them for Dundee they were always an extremely powerful side and I think this was at the back of Alex McLeish's mind when he set about building the squad at Rangers for the 2004/05 campaign.

As well as signing me, the manager had been very busy. He had secured Jean-Alain Boumsong from Auxerre in what was an amazing piece of business. He was a French internationalist but had come in on a Bosman, which left a lot of people shocked as he was being pursued by a lot of teams. My old pal Marvin Andrews was also signed on a free from Livingston. He had really developed as a no-nonsense defender and the manager was clearly bringing this pair in to build from the back.

Alex Rae was another Bosman signing from Wolves and Dragan Mladenovic came in from Red Star Belgrade. The biggest name to join up was Dado Prso. He was another player really chased by many clubs, as he was a free agent having run down his deal at Monaco. He had just played for Croatia at Euro 2004 and, having watched him in that tournament, I looked forward to teaming up with him. I hoped we could form a good partnership.

Having the Murray Park facility was excellent for pre-season. Everything was on hand for twice a day sessions, all the sports science stuff, and it gave all the new players a chance to integrate ahead of the planned trip to Austria for a training camp.

It was my first chance to work under the manager. From the first day on the training pitch I got a good feeling about Alex McLeish. He had tasted initial success at Rangers in his first two seasons, winning a couple of cup competitions and a treble, but then had to suffer a tough year. But he was a fighter. In my discussions with him when I was signing, I could see he wanted the title back badly. I didn't know much about him as a player; apart from the fact that he was a top defender with Aberdeen and Scotland. The main thing about McLeish was that he was a winner. That was so apparent.

There was a good blend with the coaching staff that supported him. Andy 'Winker' Watson was the number two. He liked a laugh with the players, but he also knew when to get serious. He was a good coach and worked a lot on the training pitches. The other coach was Jan Wouters. Again, he had been a world class midfielder with Ajax and Holland. He was quite quiet overall, but knew his stuff. I used to laugh when you would see him popping up all over the place outside Murray Park having a cigarette. But he was a bit of a fox. He took part in some of the early training games – that was when we saw the ball in an arduous start to pre-season – and he was as hard as nails. He could still play, was as fit as anyone, and he always wanted to win.

I looked at McLeish, Watson and Wouters and liked what I saw. They were good with the players, especially the new guys. The club also did everything it could to help the new faces settle in, helping out with finding houses, schools for kids, help with bank accounts and cars.

No disrespect to Dundee, but being at Rangers was a different world. But with that came expectations. I had a lot to prove as the club had chased me throughout the summer and the manager obviously had a lot of faith in me. I was determined to get going as quickly as possible and things got off to a flying start when we faced the Italian side, AS Roma, on our tour of Austria.

It was amazing and another eye-opener for me as to what Rangers meant to so many people. We arrived to face Roma in a small town, and there were Rangers supporters in large numbers mixing in with the local fans that had come out to see the game. Some of the staff at the club told me that there were a core of fans who just went everywhere with the team, didn't miss a game, no matter where in the world the team was playing. It was amazing.

There was also a huge press interest, which was different to what I was used to at Raith and Dundee. At those clubs you had maybe two or three of the local newspaper guys around every day and then a bigger interest from the national press as we got towards a game. But on this tour of Austria there were around fifteen journalists following the team, there was Rangers' own in-house media team and there were about six or seven photographers. If I didn't know how big Rangers were before, I did now!

Roma were a top team in Italy, but we were determined to win the match even if it was just a friendly. At the back for them was Philippe Mexes, who had arrived from Auxerre for around £15 million and was a former teammate of Boumsong's. I knew I would be up against him, but

Boumsong told me how to try and play him by dropping off a bit.

I liked Boumsong right away. He was a class act. In that game, you would not have known that he was the player who cost nothing and Mexes was £15m. It looked right away that Rangers had stolen some player. But my night was also not too bad. I scored a really good goal with a right-foot shot from outside the box and then followed that up with another as we won the game 4-1.

It was just the kind of start that I needed. Pre-season is all about fitness and integration into a team, but as a striker you want to be getting in amongst the goals right away to build confidence. Given that in my career I had a tendency to feed off a goals run to get my game going, I was delighted to get off the mark and immediately show that I could score goals for this team.

After Austria, we headed to London for a match against Fulham. If I thought that the fans over on the pre-season tour had been amazing, then this was something else.

There must have been around 10,000 Rangers fans at Craven Cottage for the friendly. The new guys at the club could hardly believe what they were seeing when we came out as the sea of blue and white took over the stadium. The match was played at a very high tempo for a pre-season friendly – the Scotland v England scenario always tends to bring out an extra edge, even in a game that means nothing.

The atmosphere was superb and, when Dado scored an overhead kick late on in the game to win the match for us, the fans went crazy. Dado was quickly becoming a huge favourite. He was another player with a lot of quality, but he took the club to his heart right away. I thought to myself that, with the two of us up front, the team would be getting maximum commitment from the front-line, but I had to make sure that I kept my place. The chances of that increased further when we beat Spurs 2-1 at Ibrox in the midweek, both Dado and myself scoring in what was another superb friendly game.

I was thoroughly enjoying the pre-season matches as we were coming up against such good opposition. We then headed to Newcastle for a weekend tournament – backed again by an astonishing 10,000 fans – to play the host city and Feyenoord. Everything was being geared towards the Champions League qualification matches, which would come just three days after the start of the SPL.

Unfortunately, the draw in Switzerland was not kind to us. We were paired with CSKA Moscow. In the past, teams from Russia, whilst never easy, were always viewed as being stubborn but beatable. But now, with a huge influx of oil money, the teams in Russia were spending fortunes. CSKA had a lot of foreign players, including some Brazilians like the highly rated Vagner Love, a striker who was earning a fortune playing in Moscow. We knew it was going to be extremely difficult to get into the group stages but the pressure would be on us as Celtic had earned direct qualification and all the riches that went with that as their additional prize for running away with the league championship.

The club had also been in the Champions League the season before against Manchester United, Stuttgart and Panathinaikos. It was the arena we all wanted to play in but there was nervousness about the place because of the fact we had such a huge obstacle in front of us. Everyone knew CSKA would be a very big nut to crack.

I was surprised when the SPL decided to send us to

Aberdeen on the first day of the season – especially as we had a trip to Moscow in midweek for such a crucial match. It was crazy scheduling, I thought, but as I was to discover later, the people who run the game didn't always appear to be helping teams who were trying to enhance the reputation of the Scottish game on the European scene. So we headed to Pittodrie for my first league game as a Rangers player.

I was aware that there was a long-standing rivalry between the clubs. From the minute we stepped off the bus to go into the ground, you could sense the intensity; I would probably say it bordered on hatred. They were desperate to derail Rangers on the first day, as we had new signings and big things were expected. It was a fraught match, with every ball contested like it was a World Cup Final. I got an early look at how much teams wanted to beat Rangers. And their fans? They just shouted and screamed and bayed. It was a tough, tough match but neither side could score a goal. Not a good start, dropped points on the first day.

Then it was on to Moscow. It's a really interesting city with vast streets and a collision of cultures where you can walk across from Red Square and the Kremlin to just round the corner and find a McDonald's and a Pizza Hut. We knew it was going to be extremely difficult to take a result back to Ibrox that would give us a chance of getting into the group stages, but the mood amongst the players was upbeat.

One of the first problems I felt we would encounter was the playing surface at the CSKA stadium. We trained on it the night before the game and it was a kind of synthetic surface, not full astroturf, but in-between grass and plastic and it was difficult to get a true feel for the ball. I felt it would give the Russians an advantage and they started the game on the front foot, forcing us back. Early doors, I could see they were a good side with excellent movement, a good touch on the ball and very pacey. It was no surprise when they went in front after just five minutes as they had pressurised us hard from the start.

But, as we struggled to get to grips with the pitch and the game, we started to play a bit better. I managed to get on the end of a through ball and, at the second attempt, found the net for my first Rangers goal just before half time. It was a huge moment for me as I raced away to salute the small band of our fans tucked away in the corner of the stadium. An away goal. That could be priceless if we could manage to take a 1-1 back to Glasgow. And, on a personal level, I had got off the mark. Not only that, it was on the European stage in a game that was massive for the club.

Unfortunately, the manager's half-time words not to get caught napping early doors after the break didn't hit home. CSKA made it 2-1 just moments into the second period and we could not get at them after that. So we made the long trek back home the next day with plenty of hope. 2-1 down was not the worst in an away match in Europe, but we had seen plenty of signs that they were a dangerous outfit. It would take a huge performance, we knew deep down, to get us past them.

One big blow was the loss of Alex Rae for the second leg. He had been involved in an incident with one of their players called Duda. As he lay on the ground after a challenge, Alex tried to boot the ball away and kicked him on the head. The referee saw it at the time but he was only given a yellow card. But UEFA used video evidence to look again at the incident and, to our astonishment, Alex was given a five-game ban for serious misconduct.

Now, having trained with Alex and seen him close at hand, I knew he was a hard guy. But he was not dirty. He would have run through a brick wall for Rangers, but it was way over the top from UEFA. Alex was incensed, and I felt for him. He went to Switzerland with the officials from the club to try and appeal the decision but it was upheld. A five game ban, starting in the second leg, which would mean he would miss four games in Europe after that, no matter what competition we ended up in. I thought it was a really, really harsh sentence. Alex was gutted.

There was no doubt we missed him big time in the return. After thrashing Livingston and Hibs at Ibrox we were set up nicely for the Russians' visit and we knew what we had to do. A 1-0 win and we would be into the Champions League, where we all wanted to be. But with Alex missing we lacked bite in the middle of the park. Dragan Mladenovic was called in, but he had been struggling with injury problems more or less for the whole pre-season and wasn't match sharp. Against CSKA, who were well into their domestic season, that was always going to be a problem.

With an hour on the clock, Love struck and put them 1-0 up. Our task had just become very much harder. Although we gave it everything, and Stevie Thompson got a late goal, we never really looked like knocking them out. It was a crushing night. I remember sitting in the dressing room afterwards and it was like a morgue. The draw for the group stages was the next day and we would not be in that hat. Celtic would be. They had the big time European nights coming again. We had to settle for going into a new-look UEFA Cup with group stages. It was no consolation.

Toughest thing of all was that we had to go to Parkhead

76

on the Sunday for the first Old Firm clash of the season and my first taste of the Glasgow derby. I felt for our fans right away. I knew they would be taunted about us not being in the Champions League, whereas Celtic were. It was a really tough blow for a new set of players to try and handle. We knew there would be pressure coming to Rangers, but not making the promised land of European football would just crank it up a few notches further. And now it was headfirst into the lion's den. The heat was on us all – the players and the manager.

Rangers' record at Parkhead was atrocious. They hadn't won there for over four years and it was something of a monkey on the team's back. It had become the case that the support travelled across the city more in hope than expectation.

The signing of Juninho, the Brazilian midfielder, from Middlesbrough, had also boosted Celtic. That had happened on the day of our departure to CSKA and he was a big name arrival for them. As they flexed financial muscle on us again, that only served to intensify the spotlight we were under.

Alex McLeish and the coaches did all they could to lift the heads. He based things on the principle that an Old Firm game would be the best one for us to bounce back as it was not an occasion for feeling sorry for ourselves. We had to be up for it. Our fans deserved nothing less. Sure, we were floored with the CSKA Moscow result, but we had a chance to make some kind of amends. The SPL was always the main priority, even though we were all fully aware of what the Champions League meant – on and off the pitch – to the club.

I always get nervous before games. I think if you don't have that feeling of anxiety then something is wrong. I had been to an Old Firm game at Hampden and sensed the enormity of the occasion right away. But to have the chance to play in one? That was something else. The night before the game we went to a hotel to keep everyone focused. Every player is different, some like to sit and play cards down in the lounge areas, other prefer just to be in their room watching TV or maybe playing a game-station. There are also guys who like to share rooms, others like to room themselves. It all depends on the individual. I always like my own room just to be by myself. I knew what Parkhead meant to the fans and I wanted to be ready.

I had played at Parkhead for Dundee so I knew the stadium, but going out in a Dundee strip was totally different to a Rangers strip. We got the usual warm welcome as the team bus pulled up outside the front door. We had music blaring on the bus to get the adrenaline flowing as we made the short journey from our hotel. But as we filed off the coach one by one, we knew this was not going to be a day for the faint-hearted, though I remained confident that we had the character in the team to get a result. We had been playing reasonably well.

The game started in typical Old Firm fashion, with tackles flying in. But it was very even. I didn't think we were really under that much pressure, even if Celtic had the better chances, as you would expect with them being the home side. But as so often can happen in these derby games, there was a huge sting in the tail. With five minutes to go, Alan Thompson picked up the ball around thirty-five yards from goal and smashed in a shot that dipped and swerved all the way over Stefan Klos and in off the underside of the bar. I just sank to my knees. The stadium – well the vast majority of it anyway

– went wild. It was a superb strike from him; a goal out of nothing. By the time we had tried to get back on our feet the final whistle went.

Again, in the changing room, things were tough. Just three weeks into the season we had missed out on the Champions League, lost the first Old Firm game through a last-gasp wonder-goal and Celtic had already moved five points clear. I have been asked a few times about how we felt. I'll be honest; we were reeling at that start. It was then that the manager, who was himself coming under major fire, had to try and stay calm and get the heads up. I felt for him. And the fans. The summer, with all the transfer dealings and good signings, was supposed to be the dawn of a new challenge. But as we headed into the two-week international break we were already enveloped in a dark cloud. I had scored just one goal, the strike in Moscow, and my head went down. It was no time for moping, but, as usual, I was carrying the weight of the world on my shoulders.

The shutdown for a couple of weeks gave the manager the chance to work with us on a few things behind closed doors at Murray Park. It was the first time I got a real insight into Alex McLeish as it had been so frenetic since I had signed, travelling here there and everywhere and then straight into the start of the season.

After a barren campaign the year before, he was always going to be under major scrutiny. I have no doubt he was feeling that, but he shielded it well from us. He knew there were half a dozen or so new guys and we had to settle. And the last thing a squad needs to see is the manager panicking. He stuck to what he believed, told us to do the same, and worked as hard as he could with Jan and Andy on the training pitch. But if we thought things were tough, they were just about to get even worse as our season lurched headfirst into yet more chaos.

By the time we resumed against Hearts, Celtic had opened up the gap to eight points after winning on the Saturday. We went to Tynecastle on the Sunday with a trip to face the Portuguese side, Maritimo, looming midweek.

Hearts, as always, were well fired up and we battled out a 0-0 draw. The gap at the top was now seven after five matches and some people in the media said, even that early, we would struggle to make it up. I found that crazy, but then again we were shipping points and looking vulnerable. It had to stop. Something had to kick start our season.

We hoped that would come in Madeira when we went back into European action. This was the first of two legs that could see us make it into the new group stages of the UEFA Cup. It was never going to be the Champions League, but it was a guarantee of four games and it was money that the club needed.

We knew little about Maritimo. Andy Watson was sent to watch them and the pre-match preparations were thorough, but we had another nightmare. I missed some good chances, we lost the game 1-0 and the early season problems were now being branded a crisis. On the flight home I was as low as I had been. The fans who had travelled over there – spending their hard-earned money – made it very clear they were unhappy with the performance and the result. They were spot on. For Rangers, this was simply not good enough. We spoke as a group of players at Murray Park. We had to sort it out.

I was unhappy with my own form. I had gone five games without a goal and was grilling myself in my own mind.

'Could I do more? What was going wrong? Was I maybe even trying too hard?'

It became half-a-dozen matches without a goal as we squeezed past Inverness to at least relieve the tension a bit and get two points back on Celtic after they drew with Hibs the day before, but the manager then took the decision to stick me on the bench. I was gutted. I wanted to help the team turn things around, but I knew that he was trying to freshen things up and get a reaction. I had felt things were beginning to click between Dado and myself, but Shota Arveladze and Stevie Thompson could also play up top and the gaffer explained to me that I would be taken out to try and rebuild my confidence a bit. I wasn't happy. But I understood his motives.

I always had a mental note about 26 September. It was the day I would return to Dens Park.

We ran out eight points adrift and knew it was win or bust. Dundee made things extremely tough as the clock ticked on. With twenty-five minutes to go, Alex McLeish told me to get stripped. I had already taken a fair bit of stick from the home fans, which I expected. That is a part of football and they were not going to forgive me for forcing my move to Rangers a few months before. I didn't blame them, or run onto the field with the intention of shutting them up. I was more concerned about trying to get us the points, as we simply could not afford another slip-up.

With twelve minutes to go, a cross came over from the left and Chris Burke teed me up on a plate. It was an easy finish and I wheeled away in delight, rushing over to jump on the gaffer at the touchline. You could almost see the pressure lifting there and then from him – and me! Two minutes later

I scored again to seal a 2-0 win on my former patch. It was a good feeling, but only because I had ended my barren run and we so badly needed that win. I still had a lot of time for Dundee and the fans.

I hoped, as we travelled back, that would be the turning point for me and the team. But, looking back on that first season at Rangers, I'd say the events of the following Thursday night was the spark that got the season going.

We hosted Maritimo in the return leg, needing to turn around a 1-0 deficit. We were playing for huge stakes. Had we gone out, Europe would have been gone for the season. We would have exited two competitions inside a month. Unthinkable.

It was a very, very tense night as we battered away at their well-drilled back line. Then, with twenty minutes to go, big Dado got the goal we needed. It was game on. But we couldn't find a winner and it went all the way to penalties.

The stadium was on a knife-edge. I had missed a chance to seal the game just before the end of normal time, but I walked up to take the first spot kick for us. I hit it well enough, but the keeper read it, got over and pushed his hand onto the ball. As Ibrox held its breath, the ball squeezed over. I had never experienced drama like it in my life, but I thought Stefan Klos, a world-class goalkeeper, would bail us out. And he did.

It all came down to Gregory Vignal after Maritimo missed. He calmly struck home his penalty and the place went crazy. We were through. After the match, I sensed something in the dressing room. We were hardly into the new season, but we had been battered already. But there was spirit there. I saw winners. I think that night saved our season. And maybe mine.

I spoke with the manager and asked him to trust me; trust

the fact I had my confidence back. And he did. In the next seven games I scored seven goals as Rangers started clicking into the groove. Over that spell we thrashed Amica Wronki 5-0 in the UEFA Cup and hammered Aberdeen by the same scoreline at Ibrox. We were bang in the title race again as we strung results together and Celtic shipped points. By the first week in November we had reduced their seven point gap to four. It was game on again.

I always knew that the double header we faced against Celtic in November would shape our season. We had them twice in the space of ten days – both matches at Ibrox – in the quarter final of the League Cup and the second SPL match of the season.

The cup-tie was a fantastic night and one that gave us our first taste of success in an Old Firm game. Having gone 1-0 down we showed tremendous resilience to level through Dado Prso and then win the match in extra-time when Shota Arveladze scored the winner. Afterwards, the gaffer told us in the dressing room that we had proved to ourselves that we could beat them. The mental barrier had gone and there was no reason why we could not use the momentum, the springboard of that result to kick on. We skipped out of Ibrox that night. At last we had given our fans something back.

The following weekend we faced Hibs at Easter Road and it was to prove a very eventful match for me. Midway through the first half I tangled with their midfielder, Craig Rocastle. There was nothing at all in the incident and no one even raised an eyebrow – but the assistant ref decided to raise his flag. He shouted the ref, Willie Young, over to the touchline in front of the Hibs fans and they had a short chat. To my astonishment, Young came over towards me, said I had kicked the player deliberately and held up a red card. I could not believe what I was hearing or seeing. If I do something that deserves a red card – and there have been a few moments of madness – then you need to be man enough to take the consequences. But this was a scandal. I was raging.

As I trooped off it immediately came into my mind that I would be suspended for the next league game – Celtic at Ibrox. I was almost in tears. Thankfully, Dado scored a penalty to win the game 1-0. But that didn't make up for my anger. I spoke with the management team right away and asked that we appeal the decision all the way. It was never a sending off in a million years and when I saw the TV pictures at home that night it just got worse. I called the boss and said: 'Have you seen the pictures. It's a joke.'

He agreed and the club informed the SFA that they wanted the incident referred to an appeal. It was a dreadful few days for me as I waited to hear what would happen. But, in an act of common sense, the panel found in my favour. The red card was overturned. I was clear to play against Celtic.

There was always going to be an extra edge to the second instalment of our derby double header but I don't think anyone could have predicted how crazy it would be. We were well fired up. In the dressing room beforehand the boys had got really pumped up as we knew it was the chance to claw Celtic's lead back to a point just a couple of months after people had written us off as no-hopers.

We started well. I almost scored in the first minute, but in the fifteenth minute of the match I was presented with a chance to grab my first Old Firm goal. A cross came in from the right and I took a good first touch. As Joos Valgaeren dived in towards me I skipped away from him. He cleaned me out. It was as clear a penalty as you'll ever see. I got up, above the din, and just grabbed the ball. This was my moment. Taking a deep breath I spotted it. A few steps back, picked my side. Run up and slam. I gave Magnus Hedman no chance and I was off. What a feeling.

Around me 44,000 Rangers fans were going crazy and my teammates were chasing me to celebrate. I don't think I'll ever forget how good that felt. We took a huge surge from that goal and Dado scored a powerful header twenty minutes later to have us two goals up. We were cruising and Celtic did not like it. They had banked on coming and giving us another slapping down; there had been chat from them that we could have the League Cup win, as they would win the one that mattered. I could see some of them beginning to lose it a bit. Alan Thompson, who was always a fiery character, got involved with Peter Lovenkrands. Their heads came together and Peter went down. Straight red card. Celtic were down to ten men seven minutes before half time.

There was major bad blood. Derby games can create that, but this one was threatening to boil over. In the tunnel as we went in at half time there was all sorts going on. Some of the Celtic players tried to get at Peter, who they felt had gone down too easily, and there were stewards, officials and everyone trying to keep it calm. But, not long into the second half, Chris Sutton picked up his second booking for a stupid handball and he walked as well. I think even we were in a bit of shock. Two goals up against nine men. We should have kicked on and buried the game but we were happy to see it out.

Naturally, the game caused major headlines the next day and, with some others, I found myself at the centre of the storm. There had been an incident in the second half when Stephen Pearson tackled me. TV pictures showed me catching him on the chest with my boot. To this day, I swear it was not deliberate. However, Henri Camara and myself – who was also tried by TV after he got caught kicking Gregory Vignal – were cited by the SFA and I knew there would be bother.

I don't know if the fact I had just been cleared the week before for the Hibs incident worked against me, or if it was just a case of wanting to be even in their dealings as Camara was getting done, but again, I felt it was really harsh and I went public in the press and said that there was no way I stamped on Pearson intentionally. A date was set for December for me to appear. That has always been a major bugbear of the way the rules work in Scotland. A player can be cited using TV pictures but it's a month before you're dealt with. In some cases it can be even longer. It's ridiculous as you are left with the issue hanging over you. I had to try and blank it out, no matter how aggrieved I felt. With the boost of the Old Firm win we went on a great run domestically and the goals kept coming for me.

But we made a real mess of the UEFA Cup. Having won our first two games against Amica and Graz, we then lost to AZ Alkmaar and Auxerre at home to go out on goal difference. It was a huge blow. We had the chance to have European football in the New Year but blew it.

On 14 December I was called in front of the SFA and found guilty of violent conduct for the Pearson incident. Camara was also found guilty. Due to my previous record, and the points added for that 'crime', I was handed a three-game suspension at a crucial time of the season. I was speechless. There was no right of appeal and I had to take my medicine.

That news came at a bad time and there was more to follow as we lost two massive players – one through injury, and one to the early days of the transfer window.

Jean-Alain Boumsong had been the best player in Scotland in the first half of the season. He was a class act; living up to the performances he had put in pre-season when we all admired him and felt he would be a major player. He had been linked with several clubs in England and abroad, most notably Newcastle where Graeme Souness was the manager. It was always going to be hard to keep a hold of him if they came in with big money. And our fears were confirmed. They offered over £8 million for Boumsong and Rangers had to accept. At that level of money it was impossible not to. However, when we crashed out of the Scottish Cup to Celtic after losing 2-1 at Parkhead – the first game without Boumsong – it was clear we had to act.

The manager brought in Sotirios Kyrgiakos from Panathinaikos and Thomas Buffel from Feyenoord. They were both excellent signings and looked the part right away in training. Just after we dug out a win at Aberdeen, however, we suffered another monumental blow.

Stefan Klos was taking part in a training session no different to any other. I just recall seeing him hit the deck and it was clear something had happened. He was helped from the Murray Park training field and we knew it was bad. Klos was the top keeper in the country, he was the skipper and had been a stalwart at Rangers for years. When we heard he had damaged his cruciate knee ligament and would be out for the rest of the season it sent shock waves through the club. Things did not seem to be going our way through this transfer window. Then, the real drama came.

We had been linked with Barry Ferguson for almost the entire month. I had seen him play many times before he had left for Blackburn and he was the best midfielder in the country in my opinion. I hoped we would bring him home as we really needed that kind of boost. On the final day of the window, Barry re-signed for £4.5 million to join Ronald Wattereus, the Dutch international keeper who had come in to cover the loss of Stefan. I felt it was a huge moment for us – but Celtic had also signed Craig Bellamy on loan from Newcastle and that was also a major signing, as we all knew what a good player he was. The stage was set. It was battle stations for the second half of the season.

We came flying out of the traps after the window slammed shut, destroying Dundee United 7-1 at Hampden to secure a place in the League Cup Final. Barry came on as a sub, set up a goal for me and just oozed class. The other signings had all bedded in well. I felt we looked in good shape. Three weeks later, we travelled to Parkhead for the third Old Firm clash of the season.

The teams were level on points, but it was obviously a game of huge significance psychologically. Bellamy missed a good chance early on but we played well in the game and started to take more of a grip in the second half.

With twenty minutes to go, Gregory Vignal fired in a speculative shot from well outside the box. Amazingly, Rab Douglas, the Celtic keeper, failed to deal with it and he scooped the ball up high into the net. We had the lead. With nine minutes left, a long forward pass sent me through between the two Celtic centre-backs. They got into a mess. I was clear. As Douglas raced out, I knew I had a split second to make my mind up. I looked up and lobbed the ball over his head into the net. Off I went to the corner that housed the Rangers fans. We had just won our first game at Parkhead in five years!

Many people said we had won the league that day, which was nonsense of course. We left three points clear and Celtic had a game in hand so it was hardly all over. But we took another huge surge in confidence. Week to week it was now intensity of the highest level, given the stakes. We always felt Celtic would win their games. The manager just told us to take it game by game.

In mid-March, we travelled to Dundee and won the game 2-0, but again there was a heavy price. Big Marvin Andrews had been a rock, but he damaged his knee as he landed after winning yet another header. It was ligament damage. Most players would have been for an operation right away, but Marvin refused! He told the doctors that there would be no surgery, that God would see him through it.

Now, Marvin had thighs like tree trunks and there was always an outside chance that the muscles he had built up in the upper part of his legs would protect the knee. But it was a slim chance. We couldn't believe the big man's decision. But it summed him up. He was adamant that he would not go for an operation. He did drop out of the team and missed the following week when we landed the first silverware of the season after battering Motherwell 5-1 in the League Cup Final at Hampden. I managed to get another goal and it was a great day for the fans. The gaffer said in the press the next day that he hoped the first winners' medal would kick us on for the league but a disastrous 1-0 home defeat against Dundee United saw us lose crucial ground as we headed into the run-in.

By the time Celtic came to Ibrox for the first game after the split they were two points clear – we had to win, or at least avoid defeat or it would be a long road back.

We were boosted by the return of Marvin. He declared himself fit and defied medical science to play through his serious knee ligament injury but we didn't get going at all in the first half and quickly fell two goals behind after Stilian Petrov and Bellamy found the net.

In the second half I had two great chances saved by David Marshall and when Stevie Thompson scored with a few minutes to go there was a flicker of hope. But Celtic held on to win 2-1. I trudged off the pitch, head bowed. I thought it was over. To my right the Celtic fans unfurled a banner: 'We won the league at Ibrox.' Not many people would argue against that.

The next week at Murray Park was very tough. We were five points behind with four games to go and needed massive favours from other teams. It was out of our hands. Big Marvin did some press interviews that week and said the team would 'Keep Believing'. Amazingly, Hibs went to Parkhead the following Saturday and won 3-1. We scrapped our way to a win by the same scoreline at Aberdeen the next day and the gap was back to two. Title fever had gripped the entire country. Both teams had to just keep on winning and it would go to the wire. The final Sunday of the season. We won pretty comfortably at home to Hearts and Motherwell, and Celtic beat Aberdeen and Hearts to take it to the last day. We were away at Hibs, Celtic away at Motherwell.

I think it was the longest week of my life. The infuriating thing was that it was out of our control. I used to drive into Murray Park every morning and play back some of the stupid points we had thrown away, even blaming myself for some misses. Had we just held on here, had we just won there . . . we would have had our own destiny then, I thought.

We had all adopted Big Marv's slogan. The night before the last day of the league season was spent holed up in our hotel in Edinburgh. Sure we had a lot of nerves, but it was all very calm as we knew we had to do one thing – beat Hibs and then see what happened at Fir Park. Early on in the game I was presented with a golden chance. The Hibs keeper made a mess of a clearance and I had a clear shot on goal. But I rushed it. The ball came back off the base of the post. It was around that time Celtic had taken the lead at Motherwell.

We knew we had to get a goal and win the match. The gaffer said to us at half time: 'Make them win this title. Don't give it to them. Now go out and win.' He was as pumped up as I'd ever seen him. Midway through the second period, Thomas Buffel picked up a loose ball on the edge of the Hibs box. I peeled off to his right to make an angle for the pass. Thomas was a quality player and played me in perfectly. As the Hibs defenders closed in I just tried to steer it across their keeper. It took a slight nick and slid into the corner of the net. Goal. The breakthrough we needed so badly. I went mad. I knew it could be the most important goal I had ever scored.

There was never any doubt the Rangers fans would keep us informed of events at Fir Park. It was a surreal ending to the game in Edinburgh. Hibs had nothing to play for as they had a European place secured going into the dying stages, while we had the win we needed. It all hinged on Motherwell. With a couple of minutes to go a massive roar pierced the air from the stand our fans were sitting in. Scott McDonald had scored. We all looked at the bench for confirmation. We looked at each other. We looked at the Hibs players. It was unbelievable. Barry and Alex Rae were passing the ball between them in our half of the field and were quickly told to launch it up the other end, as the last thing we needed was to concede. Then, just as we were counting down the time, there was another almighty explosion of noise. I thought, 'It's too early for the final whistle.' I looked at the bench and the signal came back. 2-1. To Motherwell. McDonald again.

We were champions. Seconds later the final whistle went and I experienced a sheer joy that I don't think will ever be matched. The drama. The excitement. Inside three minutes it had turned on its head. The helicopter with the SPL trophy had changed direction. It was coming to Edinburgh. To us. Our fans piled onto the field and we were ushered back inside. The dressing room was utter chaos. No one had given us a hope in hell – but we kept believing, just like Marvin told us to. We were all jumping around and hugging each other. It was just incredible.

Soon we got word to go out and begin the trophy presentation. Three sides of Easter Road deserted, one side bouncing. Everything I had dreamed of came true in that moment. I was a champion. Rangers had won the title back.

On the bus back to Glasgow we were treated to songs from big Dado, the coach was rocking as we drank champagne and tried to take it all in. There was nothing planned back at Ibrox, which was maybe a sign that we didn't think we would have anything to celebrate. Ironically, given the name of the man who had just delivered us the title, we sent out for forty McDonald's for all the players and staff.

The fans had flocked to the stadium as maybe only 3,500 had been at the game hours before. We went onto the pitch and there were around 25,000 Rangers supporters inside. I looked around and thought to myself. 'Look how much it means to them.'

After we paraded the trophy, the friends and family of the squad came in and we had an impromptu party in one of the Ibrox lounges. I could only have a few beers as I was booked to travel to Leeds the next morning to have surgery on the double hernia that had plagued me for the last two months of the season.

As I travelled down to England the next day, the magnitude of what had just happened began to set in. Helicopter Sunday will go down as one of the most famous days in Rangers' history. Sure, the title had been won on the last day in 2003, but Rangers had control of their own destiny that day in terms of the goals they had to score. This time, it had all turned inside minutes. Celtic had almost placed both hands on the trophy but bang, bang and it was ripped away. It had been the most amazing day of my career so far and, twenty-four hours later, even the pain of an operation couldn't wipe out how good I was feeling.

There would be big changes at Celtic, it was announced. O'Neill was standing down to be replaced by Gordon Strachan. Next year, they would come roaring back and we had to be ready. But I had scored twenty-five goals in my first season at Rangers; I had proved I could handle playing for a massive club. And, as the history books will always read, I scored the goal that helped clinch us the title in such dramatic fashion. I will always be part of Helicopter Sunday.

7

TROUBLED TIMES

Hitting the ground running was not going to be easy in my second season at Rangers. The rigours of a debut campaign had taken a lot out of me mentally, and physically, and the first part of my summer was also to be spent trying to recover from the double hernia surgery I had undergone the day after we had clinched the title at Easter Road.

I was determined, however, to prove that my twenty-five goals would be no flash in the pan, but it would be a long slog to get ready for the tough return to pre-season training and our trip to Canada where we would play a couple of warm-up games.

The manager had attempted to build on the title success by freshening up the squad. That was always the best way to improve on any success, strengthen when you are champions, and we were linked with a host of players that I kept up to date on via the internet when I was away holidaying in Spain.

Despite winning the title, qualification for the Champions League still had to be negotiated. The money the tournament generates was not guaranteed and the manager had to shop wisely. That said, he had spent big in the last January window, bringing back the likes of Ferguson and signing Buffel, so the squad was pretty strong. Shota Arveladze – a player who had a lot of skill and class – had moved back to Alkmaar in Holland, but with a European campaign of some sort guaranteed, and the title defence, the gaffer didn't want to lose too many more as we needed plenty of bodies.

He moved to sign Ian Murray from Hibs on a free transfer. I had played against him a few times and he was a tough, versatile player who I felt would be a good addition. The manager seemed to like dabbling in the French market, it had worked with Prso and Boumsong, and he had also snapped up Brahim Hemdani, the captain of Marseille, and José Pierre-Fanfan from Paris St Germain, again on a free transfer.

By the time we arrived in Toronto at the start of July, I was a bit surprised that no other strikers had been brought in. But it was then announced, whilst we were there, that Federico Nieto, an Argentine forward, would be joining up with us when we got back. I hadn't heard of him, but there was a bit of excitement about his signature. Time will tell, I thought to myself.

I always felt that McLeish would bring in extra competition up front. It was a challenge I relished, although my fitness was causing me some concern. I vowed to get back to my normal levels and doubled my sessions to make sure I would not be sidelined when the action started, giving someone else a chance to step in and making it harder for me to get back into the starting XI.

Again as the month of August moved along, the French market was plundered for Monaco's Julien Rodriguez, who was another player with a good reputation. I liked the look of the squad the manager was assembling. He was aware that his old pal, Gordon Strachan, was in place at Celtic and was spending money. That was cash that Rangers didn't have, but with the CV's that our new signings had, it looked good business.

The first challenge, of course, was to begin the season in a bit of style and make sure that we made it into the Champions League proper after the agony of losing out in the qualifiers the season before.

Once again, the draw was not kind to us. The Cypriot champions, Anorthosis Famagusta, would stand between us and the group stages. Not an easy task. They had some good players and there was the added problem of having to contend with the searing heat when we went to play them at their stadium in August.

With that task in mind, we only took on five pre-season matches, including the two in Canada. I thought that was good management as it reduced the prospect of picking up silly injuries when we had to be ready for Cyprus.

Before we had a chance to enter into the European arena, Celtic had suffered a dreadful result, losing 5-0 to the unheard of Artmedia Bratislava in the first leg of their Champions League qualifier. Despite winning the second leg 4-0, they were out of Europe and that was going to be a huge blow for them. Coupled with a 4-4 draw at Motherwell in the SPL opener, Strachan was under instant pressure. We unfurled the flag and beat Livingston 3-0, then won up at Inverness before we made the long jaunt to Cyprus.

It was incredibly hot over there. The stadium where Famagusta played in Nicosia was decent, however, and we knew it was a case of trying to get in there, get a result and get back to Scotland with our hopes intact. Famagusta showed early on they were a decent side, but I managed to scramble home a goal before Fernando Ricksen made it 2-0. We had one foot in the promised land and, even though they pulled one back, every one of us flew back from Cyprus confident we would be mixing with the big boys pretty soon. That was the ultimate aim. We wanted to be in the Champions League so badly and it was a huge thing for the club financially too.

Again the SPL computer had given us a tough fixture on our return from such a long trip – away to Aberdeen. As usual, they were pumped up for the game and we lost a late goal to go down 3-2. Their fans celebrated as though they had just won the Champions League that day which is often the way up there when they get anything from Rangers. It was a sore one for us.

But the next two games would be massive in shaping our season, home ties against Celtic and Famagusta, the second leg of our £10 million qualifier.

I had thoroughly enjoyed the Old Firm experience of the year before. Having savoured the wins and dealt with the hurt of the defeats, I had been at both ends of the emotional spectrum in terms of the biggest derby game in the world. It was everything I had expected it to be and more. With Strachan just in the door, and with Celtic having their own problems early on, it was important that we put them to the sword. As usual, the game started at a frenetic pace with a couple of half chances at either end, Celtic maybe having the better of the opening exchanges if truth be told.

Then, midway through the first half, I was to be at the centre of the first moment of major controversy. I picked up the ball just inside our half and turned to drive over the halfway line. Out of the corner of my eye I could see a Celtic player coming over at a fair rate of knots. The next thing I knew, I was just chopped down in full flight. It was Alan Thompson, a player who was never far from the heat of battle in these games. He caught me very heavily and, as I looked up from the deck, the referee, Stuart Dougal, was showing him the straight red card.

Of course Celtic were not happy, but there was nothing on my part in terms of play acting. I had been well and truly clattered and, when it was shown again on TV, Thompson didn't have much of a case as both of his feet had been off the ground. I was actually lucky not to get a bad injury.

Getting an extra man in such a huge game, so early on, is a major advantage. And we rammed that home just ten minutes later when Dado Prso volleyed in a great goal to put us 1-0 up. We had the lead, so important in derby matches. Early in the second half, we doubled that when Thomas Buffel went through to slot home and I felt the points were in the bag.

Celtic got a penalty late on to cut the deficit in half, but we were right up the park and Dado was felled. Spot kick. I grabbed the ball and tried to blank out the wall of noise. There was a bit of time left in the game and it was crucial for me to score to ensure the victory was banked. I chose my side, started the run-up and slam. 3-1. Off I went again. No better feeling in the world.

On the final whistle, it was mayhem. Neil Lennon was as passionate about Celtic as any of the Rangers players were about our team. I had already had my moments with him in Old Firm games. He hated losing. So did I. At the end of the match he was involved in a full on rammy with Dougal and was given a red card. It was chaotic and he had to be pulled away by his teammates. It had been one of those days. Old Firm games can, on occasion, just bubble away. And this one had been played right on the edge, spilling over at its conclusion.

That win gave us huge confidence for the Famagusta game. We got a solid 2-0 win and we had made it. The Champions League. But we had a shocker a few days later, losing 3-0 at home to Hibs, which was a warning that we were not to heed in terms of complacency creeping in to the title defence.

As we looked at the possible opposition in the Champions League and waited for the draw, McLeish was doing more dabbling in the market. Big Soto Kyrgiakos had been involved in a bit of a saga since the end of the title-winning season. He had only been signed on loan from Panathinaikos in the previous season, but no deal had been struck to stay at Rangers. After weeks of speculation he finally agreed to come back on a one-year deal.

Then, on the last day of the transfer window, after we had drawn Inter Milan, Porto and Artmedia – Celtic's conquerors – he brought in Franny Jeffers on loan from Charlton, Olivier Bernard on a free and, very briefly, Filippo Maniero, an Italian striker who came, trained for a few days, and then left again! That was very strange. I had a feeling that a striker would be late on the shopping list and it was Jeffers who added to the competition. I knew of him by reputation and I feared, very early on, that he might be used through the middle with his pace, with me being shunted out to the wide right berth again.

Although I knew that the team always comes first, I believed that my goals record through the middle proved that it was my better position. Deep down, I felt that it would be me, however, who would be moved around.

For all Europe provided the glitz and glamour, it was also

something Celtic would not have to contend with. They had been knocked out completely, leaving the championship as their sole aim.

I feared we would take our eye off the ball. There was something just not right about the team in the opening stages of the season and we had already lost two league games, meaning that the Old Firm win had not carried the significance that it should have. The pressure was beginning to mount as, rightly so, the Rangers fans set high standards.

When we drew 1-1 at Falkirk prior to the opening group match at Ibrox against Porto, we had dropped to fifth place in the league. That was embarrassing for the club and simply not good enough. The manager was coming in for most of the stick, as is the case at a big club. It was our responsibility to turn the performances and results around, but I could sense a difference in McLeish. He was under big pressure. We were champions, but he had the added dimension of going head to head with Strachan. They were pals from Aberdeen and the press were building it up to see who would come out on top. All of that, however, was put to one side, as we got ready for Porto and my Champions League debut.

Ibrox is an amazing stadium when it's in full voice. But that night was something special; the atmosphere, the whole sense of occasion. It was pretty sensational as we went out for the warm-up, never mind the start of the game.

I had been struggling a bit, but I had still been pitching in with some important goals. When the team for the Porto game was read out I was named as a sub, Prso and Jeffers up front, just as I had feared. It did hurt me as I felt the manager should maybe have had more faith in a player who had scored twenty-five goals the season before and done nothing wrong. Jeffers had not exactly looked brilliant since he arrived and hadn't scored. I tried not to let it bother me too much, and thankfully the game had so much it kept my mind off being dropped.

In one of the most entertaining European ties seen at Ibrox in a long while, Kyrgiakos scored a looping header with just six minutes to go to give us a 3-2 win. I had come on for the last twenty minutes and it was incredible to hear the noise and see the reaction when the winning goal hit the net.

With the huge surge in confidence from that result, we battered Kilmarnock 3-0 the following weekend. Again, I had not been named in the starting line-up and I was beginning to fear for my place.

We then travelled to Hearts, who had been absolutely flying under their new manager, George Burley. They had won seven games on the bounce in the SPL and were already eight points clear of us. This, everyone said, would be their biggest test and the day they had to show their title credentials. It was also the day I would see my season come shuddering to a halt.

Hearts came flying at us from the very first whistle. They went 1-0 up through Roman Bednar, and we were all over the place. Just before the twenty minute mark I went in for a challenge with big Steven Pressley. I had tried to shoot and he blocked it. I lost my balance and fell to the turf. Pressley's momentum carried him through and he fell over and landed right on top of me.

As he came down all his weight landed on my foot. I felt an instant, piercing pain and knew something was wrong. Despite trying to put my weight on it, there was no way I could carry on. I left Tynecastle on crutches. Rangers left with another defeat. We were eleven points adrift of Hearts before the end of September. It was shambolic. No one would say it publicly, but the title we had fought so hard for a year before was already slipping from our grasp.

I had to go for a scan the next day to get a full assessment of the injury whilst the rest of the squad headed to Italy to face Inter Milan in a match that would be behind closed doors at the San Siro because they had suffered crowd problems the year before and been hit with a UEFA punishment.

Throughout my career thus far I had been fairly fortunate with injuries but the news at Ross Hall was as bad as it could possibly have been for me. The MRI showed I had broken the metatarsal bone in my foot. I needed an operation to fix it and the prognosis was that I would be out for between ten and twelve weeks. I was absolutely devastated. The team was going through an extremely tough time and I was about to be rendered useless. Not only that, the Champions League that I had helped us reach by scoring a goal in Cyprus just a few months before, the tournament that every player wants to be in, would be over before I was able to kick a ball again. It was a total nightmare.

With some injuries, it can be hard to put an exact timescale on when you can come back. As much as I pleaded with the doctors to give me more hope, I was told that it was a set time frame for this kind of injury. The bone had to heal properly or else I would run the risk – even if I came back to training early – that I could take a whack on exactly the spot where the fracture had been and it could go again.

That injury kept me out of the first team for almost three months. I missed fifteen games. During that time, Rangers' season just went from bad to worse – domestically anyway

– and the walls were closing in on the manager. The start we had made to the championship made it almost impossible for us to even get back into the race. Even when Hearts started to falter, as people said they would, and when they inexplicably parted company with Burley, Celtic started to power into gear.

I started to attend the games with the fans. I have always enjoyed that. When you are injured, you can sit with the rest of the players who are out in a section of Ibrox for the home games. But I wanted to go and see the team for the away matches as well and would go and sit with our supporters.

As things started to fall apart, I shared their pain. It was not nice to see the team struggling to beat teams that, the season before, we had been beating with some style. We had a succession of draws and then suffered a double beating at the hands of Celtic in the space of ten days in November. We lost 2-0 in the quarter final of the League Cup, and then 3-0 in the SPL. The pressure on the manager had grown so much that people were saying he might not survive until Christmas.

Every day at Murray Park I would go in and train on my own in the gym, or do some work with the medical staff and other players who had knocks. I just felt helpless. I wanted to be out there for McLeish. He had been the man who brought me to Rangers. Even though I was unhappy at being dropped just before the injury had struck, it was my nature to fight. I wanted to fight for him and the club. The problem was that too many in the team were not doing that and the results just got worse and worse. Very soon, it became clear that Europe was all we had to hang on to. Amazingly, despite being out of the title race and the League Cup, we were still alive in our group.

The manager had held a series of talks with the chairman about his future. At one stage it looked as though he may be sacked, but Sir David Murray decided to stick with him. I felt that was the right thing to do as we still had the European situation to deal with.

McLeish had won a lot of silverware, seven trophies up until this point but, such is the way of life at Rangers, he was facing calls to be removed. He knew himself it wasn't good enough, but we still had this hope of progressing in the Champions League.

No team from Scotland had ever qualified for the knockout stages of the tournament, the last sixteen. Both halves of the Old Firm had come close in the past but, even with some very talented players in either squad, had never managed it. But here we were.

All over the place on the home front, still alive in Europe. It all came down to the last group game against Inter Milan at Ibrox in the first week of December. If we beat them, we were through. Even a draw would be enough, depending on the result of the game between Artmedia and Porto in Bratislava.

I was feeling much better and went for another scan to see if there was any way I could be back for that game. I was desperate to be available and trained as hard as I ever could to make the match against the Italians, who had already won the section.

The week before the game, none other than Luis Figo – who was still going strong at Inter – had done an interview with some of the Scottish papers saying that it would be a shame if we didn't go through, and he mentioned me as one of the players he knew about in the Rangers team. That was a huge boost for me. I re-doubled my efforts to get fit and went to see the manager for a chat.

We were on a run of nine games without a win, which was the worst in the history of the club. It was killing me that I was not available to help.

'If you need me for the Inter game, then I will be fit to play,' I said to McLeish.

'I appreciate that, Nacho,' he said. 'But the problem is you'd only be ready for the bench and the other players who have been featuring deserve to keep their place.'

I was quite surprised at this, but I suppose I could see where the manager was coming from. I wasn't really fit enough, and other guys had been there for him taking the club to the threshold of this great achievement.

I didn't get the call for Inter, which left me pretty disappointed. The manager's thinking, clearly, was that he had to stay loyal to those players who had taken the team to the position of being one game from going through, but I felt I could have been an option and I had busted a gut to try and be available. That said, it showed the loyalty McLeish had to his players.

I sat in the stand as we came from behind, with Peter Lovenkrands scoring an excellent solo goal. At the final whistle, the players waited on news from Slovakia. They had also drawn with Porto. Rangers were through. History had been made. It was an amazing sight to see the crowd at Ibrox celebrate, as they had not had much to get excited about recently, that was for sure.

Four days later I was named as a sub and came on at Kilmarnock for my first game in over three months. We had been drawn against Villarreal in the last sixteen, which meant a match against a team from my homeland. Given the teams we could have been paired with, it was an excellent draw and I felt we had a genuine chance.

From then, we had a three pronged focus; to try and finish second in the league that Celtic had taken a grip of and at least get a crack at the Champions League, to try and win the Scottish Cup and to try and get past the Spaniards into the quarter-finals when we came up against them in the February.

As soon as the transfer window opened in January, the manager signed Kris Boyd from Kilmarnock. He had built up a reputation as a goal machine and I had always been impressed with his finishing and strike rate. Again, though, he was an out and out centre forward and I knew that I would face a huge task to get back into my natural position with him now on board and Dado also in place.

In early February, we faced Hibs at home in the Scottish Cup. It was the last chance for domestic silverware, but the performance that day was to bring matters to a head. We got thrashed 3-0 at Ibrox in front of our own fans, who once again made their feelings very clear. A couple of days later, it was announced that Alex McLeish would be standing down as Rangers manager at the end of the season.

Even though my second campaign under him had been the complete opposite to the first, I felt for him. You could see the pressure that had been mounting had taken its toll. The one thing he had done was taken all the flak full on. He tried to protect the squad, when it was the players who were letting him and the team down. I hoped we would rally and at least get second spot now that his situation was clarified.

The response? We lost 2-0 to Aberdeen and 1-0 to Celtic at

home. It was just more and more embarrassment. That said, we had shown that we could raise it for Europe.

When Villarreal rolled into town we were confident that we would do something. But a 2-2 draw at home in the first leg left us with a huge task going to El Madrigal, their home stadium where they very rarely lost. In the return, Rangers played as well as we had all season. Peter Lovenkrands put us 1-0 up and we played with the kind of passion that had been missing for most of the season. They equalised early in the second half but we should have won the game and it was probably as low as I'd ever seen a dressing room at the final whistle. We had gone out of the Champions League, missing out on the quarter finals on the away goals ruling after a 3-3 aggregate over the two legs.

Two of the targets the manager had set, therefore, were gone. Out of the Scottish Cup. Out of Europe. Ten games left to try and salvage second place in our fight with Hearts.

I hadn't scored a goal since the middle of September at Falkirk and I found myself more often than not on the bench. Despite a decent run of form in the closing stages of the season, Hearts held us off. One of the worst seasons in Rangers' history had ended with a third place finish. It was simply not good enough.

Ironically, we faced Hearts in the last game of the season at Ibrox, by which time they had already secured second berth and the Champions League spot behind Celtic, who had clinched the title. McLeish was rightfully given an ovation from the fans for what he had achieved at the club.

I didn't agree with everything he did in terms of my own selection that year, but I had a lot of respect for the man. I still do. He was an excellent manager, and I will always be grateful to him for signing me. The over-riding feeling for me was that the Rangers players that season let him down. We had a squad that should have done much better and he carried the can for that.

It had been confirmed in the March that Paul Le Guen, the former Lyon manager, would be our new manager for the 2006/07 season. I looked forward to the new era and thought that it could not be any worse than the season that had just ended. How wrong I was to be . . .

8

FRENCH FIASCO

I had only read and heard good things about Paul Le Guen; a man of some standing on the European scene; a fine tactician and a strict disciplinarian. From the moment the catastrophic season before – domestically anyway – had finished there was a real sense of anticipation amongst the players about what might lie ahead under a manager with such a good reputation.

It was going to be a fresh start for everyone. I had gone through two mixed seasons under Alex McLeish and now it was time to try and impress the new man. I think many people felt Le Guen would spend big. It had been widely suggested that he would not have taken the job if there wasn't going to be a decent budget for new players. But his early dealings didn't suggest that there would be a string of big names arriving. Karl Svensson came in from Gothenburg, Libor Sionko from Austria Vienna, Lionel Letizi from PSG and some unknown French kids like Antoine Ponroy, William Stanger and a midfielder called Makhtar N'Diaye.

We had lost a fair few players from the season before, including Peter Lovenkrands, Soto Kyrgiakos, Alex Rae, Ronald Wattereus and Marvin Andrews. I feared that experience would be hard to replace with young, foreign players who knew little about the Scottish game.

The player that Le Guen had chased for a few weeks was Jeremy Clement, who had been with him at Lyon. Early on, after seeing him training, it was easy to see why Le Guen wanted him with us as he was a very good player. Yves Colleu assisted Le Guen, and a host of French back room guys who would become the new medical team and also handle the fitness side of things.

We had heard so much about him being a fitness fanatic. There had been pictures of him in the papers before he arrived doing a trek across the Sahara desert for charity, so that said enough about what we had to expect.

From the very off, I had no problem with Le Guen's fitness regime. We had very tough, double training sessions but it was not that different to what had gone on before in any other pre-seasons I have done. He was very strict about what the players ate and the menus were completely changed at Murray Park. This didn't go down well with a lot of the guys, but again it didn't bother me, as I was open to looking at new things.

There have been many theories about what went wrong for Paul Le Guen, but in the early days I have to say that I never noticed any signs that people were against the manager. He was different to what we had been used to, but that was just his way. My bigger concern was that we didn't appear to be bulking the squad up with the kind of players that you need for the SPL. I looked at some of the guys who came in and thought, 'It's OK being promising, but this is Rangers. You will not get time to settle in.'

Another observation that concerned me was that Le Guen

was not keen on tackling in training. He liked it to be played at a high tempo, but he was against any real physical contact. Now, I just didn't understand that. No one in a squad goes out to try and hurt one of your teammates in training, but you have to train the way you play. In fact, if you are too cautious in training and don't go into tackles, then it can lead to injuries. I wasn't sure what Le Guen saw in this policy, and some of the other boys – Scottish and foreign lads who were already there – agreed that it was strange. But he was the boss. What he said went.

After a couple of weeks of very tough fitness work at Murray Park we headed down to South Africa for a tour that would see us play three matches. As always when you go away over the summer, it was a time for the new players to integrate into the squad and get to know everyone. Obviously it was going to be a long flight and after catching a connection to London we faced a gruelling second flight to Johannesburg.

Some of the boys asked Yves Colleu if it would be OK to have a glass of wine to help them get to sleep on the long haul. He said that was fine. Others asked the doc for some light sleeping tablets. The plane was arranged in a two-three-two seat format. I was in the middle of the three seats section. Behind me, one row back on the left was Fernando Ricksen. For some reason, he had been seated next to a passenger who was nothing to do with the squad.

I liked Fernando. Over the two years we had been team-mates I had seen him do some mad things, but he was a boy with a heart of gold. It was hard for people who did not know him to understand some of the problems he had suffered in his life. He had a lot of family issues back home in Holland and didn't have too many people around him. Fernando was always someone who wanted to be loved, but he did have a tendency to do daft things.

I was just dozing over when I felt water splashing onto the side of my head and face. I looked behind me. Fernando had clearly been drinking heavily and was really the worse for wear. Whatever had happened, whether he had asked for more alcohol or whatever, he had become involved in an argument with the air stewardess. He had thrown some water and it had come flying over in my direction. The girl was furious and went to the front of the plane to speak to the club manager. As I was the nearest player to Fernando, the manager sent a message for me to go and see him.

Le Guen said: 'Try to relax him, Nacho. He has to calm down.' I felt it might be better for Thomas Buffel to talk with him as they were very close pals and Thomas could also communicate with Fernando in Dutch. But there was no calming him down. He had lost it completely and was ranting and raving that people would not be telling him what to do. The whole front cabin where we were was shocked. Fernando was going to be in serious trouble and he just kept shouting when whoever from the management went up and tried to get him to calm down. The manager said to him: 'Sit down, we will talk tomorrow.' But Fernando was gone.

On arrival in South Africa, we transferred to the team hotel that would be our base for the next week or so. Inside an hour or so, a meeting was called and we were informed that Fernando would be sent home on the next flight back to London and then up to Glasgow where he would train with the youth team until we got back.

I knew right there and then that Le Guen saw an opportunity to make his mark. He wanted everyone to know that he was the boss and that anyone who stepped out of line would be hammered. Fernando was the captain and a very well-liked boy. It would send a huge message through the squad, which was exactly what Le Guen was trying to do.

Looking back, there is no question that Fernando was in the wrong. He should not have been drinking heavily on that flight. It was totally unprofessional, but I still felt that Le Guen over-reacted. He could have fined him two weeks wages; he could have dealt with things in a different manner.

For all his faults in that incident, Fernando was a key player for Rangers. I knew there and then it would be over for him under Le Guen. And I was right. He was shipped out on loan for the rest of the year to Zenit St Petersburg, managed by the man who had brought him to Rangers, Dick Advocaat. There goes another one, I thought to myself. The squad was being deprived of more and more experience.

The knock-on effect from finishing third meant that we had no early season European games. We were into the UEFA Cup and would have half a dozen SPL matches before we entered that competition. For me, that should have been a bonus for a new team. OK, we all wanted to be in the Champions League again, but having a clear run at the start of the league season should have meant a solid start domestically. That turned out to be far from the case.

I came on as a sub on the first day of the season at Motherwell as we won 2-1 to get the new campaign off to a winning start. It was a decent performance and some of the new players, like Sionko who scored, had played well. But with the likes of Barry Ferguson, who was still on his way back from an ankle operation, missing from the squad, I still felt we looked a bit light in terms of numbers and experience.

Maybe Le Guen did too. He moved to sign Filip Sebo from Austria Vienna and also brought in Lee Martin and Phil Bardsley on loan from Manchester United after Sir Alex Ferguson gave them the green light to come to Scotland. They both looked like decent young players, but again I wondered if they had enough experience.

Across the city, Strachan was bringing in decent players – like Thomas Gravesen from Real Madrid and Kenny Miller from Wolves – and we didn't seem to be able to match that. Le Guen's policy seemed to be to recruit younger guys with potential. It was a gamble. And it didn't work. Successive draws against Dundee United and Dunfermline had us dropping crucial points already. The best display so far came as we beat Hearts 2-0, but that was followed up by more dropped points in a 2-2 away draw at Kilmarnock.

I was completely out of the picture as the first month of the season progressed. I feared that Le Guen just did not rate me as a player and I began to wonder if there would be a future for me at Rangers. As the transfer window got ready to close, the club accepted a bid from Coventry City for me of around £450,000. It flashed up on the TV screens at Murray Park that I was going down there to sign. News to me, I thought. I didn't want to leave Rangers.

Right there and then I had two choices; to give up and go, or to fight for my future. I went to see Ian Durrant, a man who I had become very close to over my two years at the club. Durranty had the total respect of every Rangers player, as he was a true legend, but he was also a guy who would give you an honest opinion.

'If you don't want to go, then stay and fight wee man,' Durrant said as I had a heart to heart with him about my future. I went to see Le Guen and told him that I would be staying and I would not leave the club. To be fair, he was fine. I always seemed to get on OK with him. I had been in for one or two private conversations with him prior to that talk at the end of August and I got the feeling he liked me enough as a guy, although maybe not enough as a player as I was not getting a sniff of a chance.

I told the manager I would be working harder than ever to get a place in the team. He was happy enough with that. I was not going to walk away, that would have been too easy.

We returned to action after the international break at the start of September and kicked-off with a resounding 4-0 win over Falkirk. Again, I did not feature. In the midweek, we had a trip to Norway to face Molde in the UEFA Cup match that would determine whether or not we went into the group stages.

Barry Ferguson was now back in the group. I have to be honest and say that I always liked Barry. First and foremost, he was, still is, a winner. Sure, he could be a real pain in the arse on the pitch when he was shouting and bawling at you, but that was just his style. He was a genuine class act in midfield and I felt it was going to be crucial if we were to have any chance of doing anything after such a sloppy start to get him back and in full-form.

In the training session the night before the game against Molde, Barry shouted at Libor Sionko to step it up a bit. Le Guen stopped things and called Barry over. He didn't like him shouting at the other players and told him that. For me, it was the first sign of problems.

I don't know what Le Guen's perception of Barry before that was. They had not really worked together as Barry had

115

been away with the second team and the medical staff getting his fitness back. But I had a feeling that Le Guen had no regard at all for the captaincy, or what it stood for. Barry, on the other hand, was so proud to be the skipper of Rangers, a club that he had supported all his life and been at – bar a brief spell at Blackburn – his entire career.

We drew the game 0-0 and were lucky to get away with it. Again, I was not called on and I was beginning to get really concerned about my lack of football.

On the Sunday, we went to play Hibs. They had built a side full of young, aggressive players and they just went for Rangers right from the first whistle. We were blown away really, and lost the game 2-1.

After just seven league games, we were already four points behind Celtic. The defence was giving away really soft goals. Svensson and Brahim Hemdani were now in the central area, where once it had been the likes of big Marvin Andrews and Soto Kyrgiakos, who were tall and aggressive. Teams looked at us, I thought, and saw a soft touch.

I was brought out of cold storage for only my second appearance of the season the following midweek when we beat Dunfermline 2-0 in the League Cup, which was the starter before the weekend main course – the first Old Firm game of the season at Parkhead.

Already, we were under massive pressure. The implications of defeat would see a seven-point advantage for Celtic already and the season would look as though it was going down exactly the same road as the one before.

It was a game that we never looked like doing anything in if truth were told. Two of Celtic's big summer arrivals – Gravesen and Miller – got the goals as we were brushed aside

Getting a feel for the ball . . . me as a toddler in the local park.

Mum holds me tight at my christening in 1979.

Happier times. The two ladies in my life, mum and Arantxa, just before Christmas in Dundee in 2003.

Me and Donna at my tribute dinner 14 March 2010 along with my team-mate Neil Alexander, his wife Joanne and Steven Davis.

The early days as I celebrate a goal for Raith Rovers in a win over Falkirk.

Seeing red. Ref Iain Brines sends me packing at Dunfermline in August 2002.

Just Fab. Ravanelli gives me some advice after my derby goal against Dundee United in October 2003.

Blue heaven as Alex McLeish welcomes me to Rangers after the summer of 2004 signing saga.

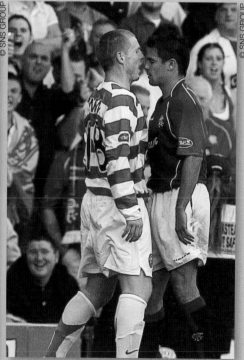

Silver lining. My first trophy with Rangers after we hammered Motherwell 5-1 in the 2005 League Cup Final.

You need a filling Neil! Myself and Lennon in a typical Old Firm head-to-head.

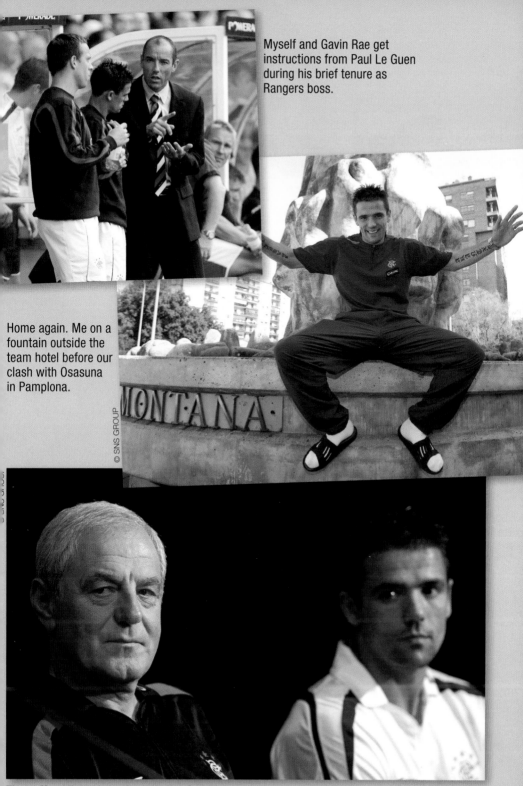

Myself and Gavin Rae get instructions from Paul Le Guen during his brief tenure as Rangers boss.

Home again. Me on a fountain outside the team hotel before our clash with Osasuna in Pamplona.

MONTANA

The gaffer. I listen intently as Walter Smith prepares to answer a question at a pre-match press conference.

The joy of scoring a goal for Rangers is never lost on me. I let the opposition fans know what I think (above), whilst it's clear to see what it meant to me scoring a crucial late winner against Red Star Belgrade in 2007. And the moment I'll never forget (right) as I slide on my knees in front of the Rangers fans after scoring the penalty in Florence that took us to the 2008 UEFA Cup Final in Manchester.

I'm part of the celebrations after we beat Dundee United in the 2008 League Cup Final but being suspended for the match after my crazy red card hurt like hell.

Myself, Thomas Buffel and my close friend Carlos Cuellar visit the Acropolis in Athens before the Panathinaikos game.

The agony of losing the UEFA Cup Final to Zenit reduces me to tears in Manchester.

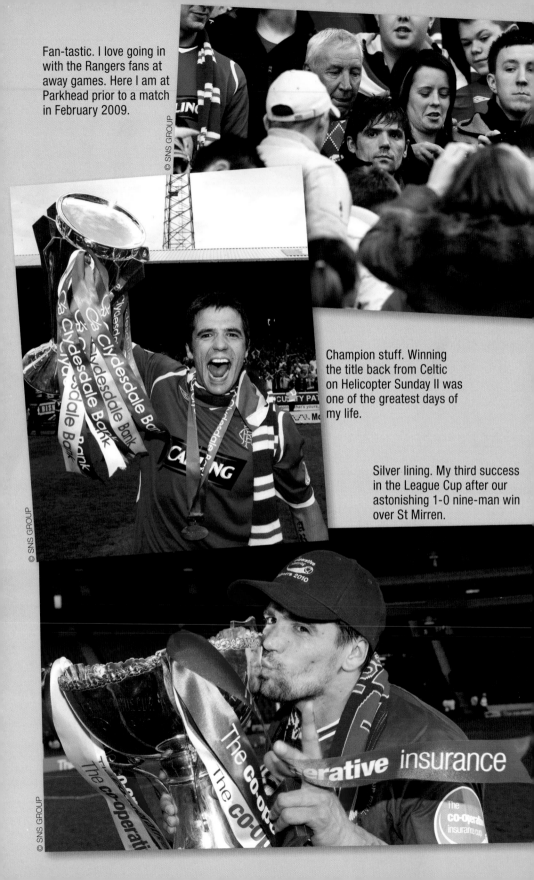

Fan-tastic. I love going in with the Rangers fans at away games. Here I am at Parkhead prior to a match in February 2009.

© SNS GROUP

© SNS GROUP

Champion stuff. Winning the title back from Celtic on Helicopter Sunday II was one of the greatest days of my life.

Silver lining. My third success in the League Cup after our astonishing 1-0 nine-man win over St Mirren.

© SNS GROUP

2-0. I looked around the dressing room at Parkhead and didn't like what I saw in terms of morale. We were all over the place again. Le Guen, the man who was supposed to lead us back to success, was struggling to get any kind of response. It was almost the end of September and, even though we did beat Molde 2-0 to make it into the UEFA Cup sections, the problems were just beginning to mount.

It has been said many times, and I have even been asked this, if there were people in the dressing room who tried to undermine what the manager was doing, if there were cliques between the Scottish and foreign guys that caused all sorts of problems.

Firstly, yes, there were people who did not agree with everything the manager was trying to change. More often than not, they would talk to Barry. As the captain, he would go to the manager and pass on the concerns. There were issues over the food he wanted us to eat and Barry would ask if it could be altered. Maybe that is where Le Guen came up with the theory that Barry had too much influence. I didn't see it, to be honest. He was just doing what captains do, as the link between the dressing room and the manager. But, as I saw right from the start, Le Guen had no regard for the captaincy.

As for cliques, the French-speaking players did stick together. That is only natural. The Scottish boys were also mates, on and off the pitch. But I saw Dado Prso, who spoke French but was also one of the boys with the home-based players, try to get the dressing room going. Being Spanish, I had no issues with anyone. I spoke to everyone. I just wanted to see the team do better!

I NEVER saw or heard anyone deliberately try to undermine the manager, or what he was trying to do. And even though people claimed that some players would go on the pitch and ignore what he had told them to do, I was never aware of that going on either.

If there was a group of players at the club that tried everything they could to get rid of the manager, and Barry and the Scottish boys took the blame for this afterwards, then I never saw it. Results, as is always the case, were his biggest enemy. Not anyone within.

As I said, I always felt Le Guen was approachable. I thought nothing of knocking on his door and asking why I wasn't playing and I did that a few times in the early months. It was down to me, he would say. I felt, looking at some of his buys like Sebo having no success at all in front of goal, that I should have been given a decent chance. And, as we headed into October, he obviously felt the same way.

After a humiliating 1-0 home defeat to Inverness Caley in the league, we had to travel to Italy to take on Livorno in our first UEFA Cup group match. The atmosphere at this stage was very tense, as the results had been dreadful. I could tell Le Guen was really feeling the pressure as points slipped away and the title looked like a lost cause again.

We set up an 11 v 11 in a training game at Murray Park the day before we left for Italy. Midway through the first half, Phil Bardsley clattered into Thomas Buffel. Now, it was a heavy tackle and maybe one that should not have been happening in a training game, but these things happen. Thomas, much as he wasn't happy and felt it, didn't make that big a deal out of it, but Le Guen stopped the game and sent Bardsley back to the changing rooms. He then told him that he would not be in the squad for Italy.

I was shocked at that. It was as if he had to again flex his

118

muscles, just as he had with Fernando. Now I am not saying that the manager's wishes should be disrespected. He banned heavy tackling from training, that was his right, but given we were in the trenches, the last thing we needed was going another player down. It also sent another nervous ripple through the squad.

I was given a starting jersey by Le Guen against the Italians and scored as we won 3-2 to become the first Scottish team to win on Italian soil. After my goal I ran over and jumped on him to celebrate. It was just one of those things that you do, it was not pre-planned. The manager needed a result, we all did. It was relief, emotion, as I hadn't been given many opportunities.

We returned home with a much-needed confidence boost. It was St Mirren away on the Sunday and I felt I would start the game after my performance in Italy. But Le Guen named me as a sub again. I was gutted. It was a tight game, St Mirren battling for every ball and making it tough as they always do, and then he threw me on. I snatched a late winner for us to escape with a 2-1 win, again doing the manager a turn.

The rest of the autumn was to follow a similar pattern. Inconsistent results, with only Europe bringing any joy as we beat Maccabi Haifa, Partizan Belgrade and drew with Auxerre to make it into the last thirty-two after Christmas.

We were beaten 2-0 at home by First Division St Johnstone in the League Cup on one of the darkest nights in the club's history and I could see Le Guen just losing more and more desire. By the time we faced Celtic the week before Christmas, the league title was gone. A late goal from Brahim Hemdani salvaged a 1-1 draw, but Le Guen came out afterwards and spoke publicly about how he didn't think a captain was impor-tant after being asked about Barry and his role in the team.

There was no doubt that the two of them had a complete breakdown in relationship at that stage. They didn't like each other, that was obvious.

The results just got worse, a 2-1 defeat up at Inverness and a 1-1 draw with St Mirren well and truly putting Rangers back into crisis.

On 2 January we were scheduled to face Motherwell at Fir Park. We had training on New Year's Day, as usual. We were all in the dressing room, it was quite quiet. The next thing Barry came in and started emptying his locker. He had been stripped of the captaincy and told he would no longer play for Le Guen. I had never seen anything like it in my life. Barry was clearly upset and didn't say much as some of us tried to find out what had gone on. He quickly left, we went out to train and it was just surreal.

That was Fernando sent packing away back in July, now Barry. Where was this going to end? News quickly leaked about what had happened and it was the last thing we needed as we went to Motherwell, always a tough place to get a result. For a few weeks I had feared that the results would start to see us fighting just to get second place again, which would have been a disaster given the need for the Champions League revenue. We had to start picking up points, but we were a club well and truly in crisis.

Some of the fans booed the manager as he got off the bus to go into the stadium. I just put my head down and went in. It was horrible, seeing Rangers reduced to this. The infighting, the tension, the press all over the club saying we were a shambles. And we were. The only bonus that day was that we won the match, 1-0. But Barry had been banished. His time, or so we believed, was over.

During the week we had a visit to Yorkhill Sick Kids Hospital to hand out some gifts to the children who were very unwell over the holiday period. A large number of the players were there. Suddenly, news started to filter through that Le Guen, Colleu and the rest of the French backroom team were loading their stuff into their cars and leaving. We were stunned. He had spoken with the chairman and it had been decided that the best option would be for him to leave. Ian Durrant was put in temporary charge of the team with immediate effect. It did not surprise me that Le Guen had had enough, but I did think he would have stayed until the end of the season.

For me, looking back on his short spell at the club, I would say he made crucial mistakes on several fronts. He was a good tactician, very professional and thorough, but he signed the wrong kind of players for the Scottish game.

He came to a massive club like Rangers and was determined – no matter what or who was in his way – to try and change the culture of the entire club and the dressing room. He took on too much, too soon. It was never going to work. As I said, for all the claims he was undermined, only others can truly answer that. If they were not giving everything for him and the club, then they would have to answer that. But I was never there when anyone, or any group, sat down and said 'right, let's do this or that' to get him out.

He should have been a good manager for Rangers but he made mistakes. It was a sad, sorry affair and not a time that the club can reflect on with any satisfaction as we again kissed goodbye to a season without as much as a challenge. Le Guen played his part in that as much as anyone else he tried to blame.

9

THE LEGEND RETURNS

The whole dressing room was in a state of shock when we reported for training at Murray Park the day after Paul Le Guen had left the club. Ian Durrant was put in charge of first team matters, which was at least some kind of continuity, most of the players knowing him from around the training ground every day in his role as manager of the reserves. Durranty called us all together and said we had no option but to focus on the here and now. Rangers had to go on – no matter the circumstances – as the club was bigger than anyone, or anything. It was just what I expected Durranty to say. He was Rangers, through and through.

The press was full of speculation that Walter Smith would be returning as manager to replace Le Guen and that he would be assisted by the greatest ever striker the club had known, Ally McCoist. I knew of both of them, not only after being told what they had achieved at Rangers, but also by the fact they had performed an amazing job turning the Scotland national team around after the disastrous Berti Vogts reign.

I felt Walter Smith would be perfect for us. We needed a man who would command respect in the wake of the Le Guen shambles. We needed a man who knew what Rangers was all about. As the man who had guided the club to nine titles in a row, he certainly knew what Rangers required.

It was a tough time. When the manager leaves it's always uncertain and we knew that the fans were looking for some kind of immediate up-turn. We only had the Scottish Cup, and a last thirty-two tie against Hapoel Tel Aviv in the UEFA Cup to look forward to as the League Championship and the League Cup were long gone.

Some of the players in the dressing room – mostly the Scottish boys who knew Walter Smith from the national set-up – told us what we could expect if he did indeed take the job, as most of the pundits were now saying he would once a deal was sorted out with the SFA. But in the midst of all the chaos that had ensued since the turn of the year, we had an extremely important cup-tie against Dunfermline to get through.

Going to a First Division club is never easy and East End Park was a venue where I had always found it tough, both as a Dundee player and a Rangers player.

Durranty was handling things on a day-to-day basis and kept the training bubbly. I think he knew the players were reeling a bit, especially the ones that had been brought in by Le Guen just a few months before, and he wanted to keep everyone's minds on the job. He knew that at any time a call could come that Walter Smith had agreed terms and he would be stepping aside, but Durranty was putting Rangers first, and told us we all had to do the same.

By the time the Friday came ahead of our Sunday trip to Fife, there was no movement on the managerial front. Durranty would be the gaffer for our Cup tie. I had so much respect for him, and not only because he had spent a lot of time lifting me from the doldrums over my two and a half years at the club.

I had seen some footage of him playing on DVD and also heard from people who had been at the club for years that Ian Durrant was a midfielder way ahead of his time, a box-to-box man who could score goals and would have been destined for a career at one of the top clubs in Europe had he not been cruelly set back by a shocking tackle from Neil Simpson at Aberdeen back in 1988. He was everything that a Rangers player should be and I looked up to the example he set. With this likely to be his one and only game as Rangers manager before the new boss arrived, there was no way I wanted to let him down.

Unfortunately, that is exactly what we did that day at Dunfermline. I felt pretty ashamed afterwards as I looked at his face. We had one game to get through before the new era dawned, but we failed miserably. We had hit real rock bottom.

No disrespect to Dunfermline, but they should not have been living with Rangers. But, after some quite woeful defending, they found themselves 3-0 up just minutes into the second half of the match. It was yet another complete embarrassment. We rallied in the game and got it back to 3-2 with two goals from Kris Boyd, but could not find an equaliser and we were dumped out of the second cup competition of the season by another First Division side.

Afterwards, Durranty said to the media: 'I think the new manager saw today just what a huge task he has on his hands.' He didn't need to say anything to us after the game or on the way back. The hurt on his face said it all. We had let him down. Big time.

On the Tuesday, we reported for training at Murray Park

to be met by two new faces – Ally McCoist and Kenny McDowall. A deal had been done for Rangers new management team to take over and they were in charge of training whilst Walter Smith went to hand in his resignation to the SFA, who had refused to let him leave as a compensation package had yet to be agreed with Rangers.

I liked their style right away. The training was sharp and they tried to get a spirit working in the group immediately as we all waited on Walter Smith's arrival. I didn't know anything about Kenny, but obviously Ally McCoist's reputation spoke for itself. He had been a true legend, scoring hundreds of goals over a fifteen-year spell at the club and I thought that it would be a huge benefit for me to have someone with his standing in the game now working with me on all aspects of a striker's game.

Walter arrived that morning and called a team meeting. He was a man who, when he walked into a room, commanded instant respect, a figure like Sir Alex Ferguson in that regard. He told us what had gone on before would not count and that it was a fresh start for everyone.

The main aim, he rammed home in no uncertain terms, was to get some pride back into our performances, to ensure that we finished second in the SPL and therefore earned a crack at the Champions League again, and to try and advance as far as we could in the UEFA Cup. There was an aura about him. He was a real manager in every sense of the word. He made you want to play for him.

There was an instant reaction to Walter's arrival on the Saturday when we thrashed Dundee United 5-0 with one of the best performances we had produced for many seasons.

The thing he knew was that we had to become hard to beat

again. I had a feeling that some of the foreign lads would move on and many of them, like Julien Rodriguez, Jeremy Clement and Lionel Letizi, opted to go almost instantly. Some of them had bought into the so-called Le Guen revolution and didn't fancy it any more. It was right for them and it was right for Rangers. We only needed people in the squad who were absolutely ready to buy into what the new manager wanted.

The centre of defence had been a major issue for the entire season. There was a time when almost every basic ball lobbed into the box was either costing a goal or leading to a near thing. Walter Smith moved quickly to bring in Ugo Ehiogu, the experienced former England and Aston Villa defender. He was a big six-foot-plus, no-nonsense stopper – just what we needed. He then snapped up Davie Weir from Everton, another very experienced defender whom he had worked with at both club and country level.

They shored up the back-line almost instantly and we started to get clean sheets, or would lose just one goal in games, giving ourselves a real chance to take something from matches that earlier in the campaign had been slipping away through basic errors. Kevin Thomson – who was the captain of Hibs and one of the best young midfielders in the country – also came in for £2 million.

We faced a tricky first leg in Israel when the European campaign resumed in February. Hapoel would be a stern test, but we now had a far more solid look about our team and the manager's influence was telling.

However, that night in Tel Aviv I saw the angry side of Walter Smith for the first time. We didn't play at all well in the first half and lost a sloppy goal just before the break. The manager was simmering at half time. I could see in his eyes he was not amused with what he was seeing. He demanded more from us, and said we would go out of the competition unless there was a major improvement. We knew this was not a man to be messed with.

Eight minutes after the break I managed to pounce from close range to draw us level at 1-1. But it was never a game that we had control of, and we came under late pressure and fell behind 2-1 with about fifteen minutes to go. Hapoel saw it out and celebrated at the end as if there was no second leg!

Upon entering the dressing room, it was clear the manager was not amused with what he had just seen. He was about to explode, but waited until we got back to the hotel before calling all the players to a meeting. Walter Smith stood and addressed the players as we sat in stony silence. 'Right, this is a big club and perhaps some of you don't seem to understand how big,' he rasped.

'There are two options for each and every one of you in this room. Those who want to be a part of the future, who want to play for Rangers, they have to give this club more than what I saw tonight. And if there are those who don't want to be a part of it, who don't want to give us everything, they can just f—— off right now. There is no place here for you.'

I have to say he was a very scary man in that mode. Not a word was said back in response. A month into the job we had seen for the first time the side of Walter Smith that came out when he felt people were dipping below the standards expected of a Rangers player.

Eight days later, in front of a big Ibrox crowd and with a place in the last sixteen of the UEFA Cup on the line, we hammered the Israelis 4-0. From the first whistle we went after them and never relented. It was just what the manager had demanded.

In the next round, we came up against Osasuna – another trip back to Spain for me. There was a big media interest in the game from my own country and I would get calls from various Spanish papers and radio stations asking me for my thoughts on the game. The first leg was in Glasgow and I knew from my contacts back home that although Osasuna were not regarded as one of the famous teams in La Liga, we would have to play very, very well to get past them.

They proved to be a tough nut to crack and took the lead at Ibrox. They were well organised, extremely comfortable on the ball but we never really got into the groove and needed a very late goal from Brahim Hemdani to snatch a 1-1. The game took a fair bit out of the legs, but just three days later we had to head for Parkhead.

The press had been building this one up for weeks. More often than not in his first spell as Rangers manager, Walter Smith had enjoyed the upper hand in Old Firm games. Now Celtic were ruling the roost again. The game meant nothing in terms of the title, as that was long gone, but it was about pride. The manager drummed that into us every day before we made the short journey across the city.

Celtic had the better of the chances that day but, midway through the second half, big Ugo Ehiogu threw himself into the air as the ball bobbled around from a corner and sent an acrobatic bicycle kick shot past Boruc into the top corner of the net. 1-0 Rangers. The Celtic players looked a bit dazed at what was happening. We saw it out and won the third Glasgow derby of the season. All we did that day was give our fans something back – and leave a small reminder to Celtic and their supporters that next time around it might not be as easy for them. Rangers would be coming back off the deck. There was no question of that.

As is the way in football sometimes, we went from that high to a painful low just a few days later in Spain. At 1-1 from the first match, it was always going to be a stern task against Osasuna on their home patch. There was plenty of effort, but not enough craft and we lost the match 1-0 to go out of Europe.

With the points now coming in, that would help us ease away from the rest and assure second spot. But it was season over again by mid-March. That was tough, at the business end of the campaign you want to be winning trophies, or at least competing, but we were left to watch once more as Celtic clinched their second consecutive title. When we faced them after the split at Ibrox, there was nothing once more to play for but pride and some bragging rights for our fans. We were far more up for the match than Celtic and beat them quite easily 2-0. At the end, Boruc raced up and grabbed a 'champions' flag from the Celtic fans before waving it around. He was like that at times, and tried to rub our noses in the fact that it had been two Old Firm wins in a row, but it meant nothing in terms of a title.

That was the aim, as one of the most turbulent season in the club's history ended. For two seasons we had been no more than nuisance value in the championship battle. But we had the legend back at the helm. It was time for Rangers to come out fighting.

10

ROAD TO MANCHESTER

The European scene always seemed to bring out the best in me. Over the years, I think the fans began to look at me as someone who was a bit of a lucky charm, something of a talisman when Rangers came up against continental opposition. I certainly enjoyed a fair few nights when things ran for me and seemed to find myself amongst the goals, which is something people can never take away. It's amazing when I chat with the fans I meet about my career or favourite games; they can all instantly recall some of the goals in the Champions League or UEFA Cup. That makes me very proud, as I am up there amongst some very illustrious names in terms of the club's scorers in European competitions.

The 2007/08 campaign turned out to be one of the most momentous in the Rangers' history and it also fills me with great personal pride looking back on what we achieved, and what I managed to do personally. When things kicked off at the end of July, no one associated with the club envisaged what would unfold, what an amazing journey we would go on over the next nine months or so.

After finishing as runners-up in the SPL, we knew it was going to be a tough task to get into the Champions League group stages. We would have to negotiate two qualification rounds, four games in total, to be in there with the big boys again, but it was a challenge we just had to meet head on. The dangerous aspect for Scottish teams is that the qualifiers come very early in the season. You have not kicked a ball in anger in the league and find yourself pitched into these high-tension matches that are worth in excess of £10 million to the club. There is major pressure on the players as so much is on the line.

We managed to overcome all of that and get there . . . but this was a journey that led us all the way from Montenegro to Manchester. A journey I will never forget, even if it didn't end the way I had dreamed . . .

CHAMPIONS LEAGUE QUALIFICATION
RANGERS 2 ZETA 0
31 July 2007

Our first match on the road we hoped would lead to the Champions League was at Ibrox against Zeta, a team from Montenegro. Their country had recently gained independence from Serbia, and we knew that teams from that part of the world would be tough to break down and have technically gifted players. On a muggy Glasgow night, that proved exactly to be the case. The atmosphere was very tense as the crowd knew exactly what was on the line. The perils of these kinds of matches had been borne out a couple of years before when Celtic were dumped out by Artmedia, a team no one had ever heard of.

There was no safety net of the UEFA Cup at this stage; that only opened up if we made it to the next round and the tension ran through the team and stifled our performance.

The fans booed us off at half time after a pretty poor display. I came on as a sub at the break and the gaffer told me to be direct and try to get in behind them. We managed to scramble a lead through Davie Weir, but Alan Hutton was then sent off for a daft second yellow card. They just sat deep, but we did get another goal from Lee McCulloch to get a decent first leg cushion.

ZETA 0 RANGERS 1
7 August 2007

I had never heard of Podgorica, never mind visited the place. But we knew we had to get in, get the job done and get home. With a 2-0 lead it was a case of trying to keep things tight and offer them no encouragement. Again I was on the bench, which gave me the chance to witness close up one of the ugliest parts of football – crowd racism.

We had two black players in our team, Jean-Claude Darcheville and DaMarcus Beasley. What happened that night was disgusting. When they touched the ball there were monkey noises made from sections of the home crowd. It was dreadful to see that happening to your teammates. In Spain, there had been some issues with black players being abused so it happens in the so-called elite countries as well. But I felt for the two lads. Beasley rammed the noises right back down the morons throats when he slotted a goal with ten minutes left to kill the tie. Job done.

RANGERS 1 RED STAR BELGRADE 0
14 August 2007

I was frustrated that the gaffer left me on the bench again for this game. Red Star had a famous reputation and had won the old European Cup so we knew it was going to take a huge performance from us to get through to the group stages. Again, you could feel the tension in the air. I think the fans sensed how huge a night it was, but again we didn't really cope with the demands of that and the performance was scrappy, without any chances really being created.

With twenty-five minutes to go I was pitched on alongside Daniel Cousin as the manager tried to shake things up. To be honest I didn't think a goal would come. But in the last minute, I latched onto a flick-on and smashed a shot into the bottom corner of the net. It was a great feeling, one I had enjoyed before in Champions League qualifiers when we had faced CSKA Moscow three seasons before, and then also Famagusta. As I walked off at time-up, I hoped this goal, unlike the one against the Russians, would make a difference like it had in Cyprus and help carry us through.

RED STAR BELGRADE 0 RANGERS 0
28 August 2007

Belgrade was an intimidating place. There was no doubt they fancied it against us big time. The night before the match we trained at the Marakana Stadium and there were riot police all over the place – and there was no crowd to keep an eye on! A couple of the lads had played in the ground before and said it would be wild when the action got going for real. It was a very nervous time for everyone. The manager, the directors and the players – we knew what was at stake in terms of finance and also prestige. We had police cars out in front of the team bus, and behind, as we snaked our way through Belgrade to the ground.

We were there very early for the match – and there were thousands of Red Star fans already milling around. When they saw the team bus they were all surging forward and going crazy. The police had to hold them back. It was a very old stadium, shaped like a bowl. The dressing rooms were set back behind one end, and you had to walk down a dark tunnel to get to the pitch. When we went out to have a look at the surface, there was a line of riot police on either side of the tunnel. It was like a scene from Star Wars. They looked very menacing with the full gear on, helmets with the visors open, shields in hand and huge batons. I didn't want to look at any of them in case they growled back!

I had never seen anything like it when we went out for the warm up. The stadium was almost full, they were whistling, going crazy and throwing things. The noise was unbeliev-able. Behind the goal, flares were going off and then there was some fighting – we later found out that factions in the Red Star support fight with each other – which the police had to wade in to sort out.

As the teams went out side by side for kick off I looked up to see this wee pocket of Rangers fans, maybe around 1000, tucked away in the corner with huge empty areas of seats on either side of the fences that had been erected in the away fans area. There were probably as many police looking out for them on either side of the empty areas. When the game got underway, it was one of the most fraught nights I had ever been involved in.

Again I was benched, but I could see the boss wanted to keep it tight and then maybe keep some attacking options for later on. We had to ride our luck at times, and rely on brilliant goalkeeping from Allan McGregor. But we got there. It was fantastic in the dressing room as we all celebrated and it sank in. We had a lot of new players who would be sampling the Champions League for the first time – for me it was going to be the second. It was a great flight home!

CHAMPIONS LEAGUE GROUP STAGES

There is nothing better than the anticipation of the Champions League draw. Just seeing your team's name in amongst the cream of the continent is a fantastic feeling for the players and, more importantly, the fans.

I remember speaking to some of our supporters about how they would sit and watch the Champions League draw from Monaco live on Sky Sports, with their laptops switched on. As soon as the draw came out, they would start sourcing flights right away for the three away matches in the group to try and get the best deals! And neither us, nor the fans, were disappointed when Rangers tumbled out of the hat.

It was dubbed the 'Group of Death' when we drew Barcelona, Lyon and Stuttgart. But for me it was a dream. That is what you want in the Champions League, to test yourself against the very best. And the fact I grew up supporting Real Madrid gave the prospect of facing Barcelona an extra dimension!

RANGERS 2 STUTTGART 1
19 September 2007

If you are to have any chance of progression in the Champions League then winning your home games is absolutely crucial. We knew that Stuttgart would be a very tough team to get a win against. German outfits are never easy. It was clear that the manager favoured a 4-5-1 system in Europe. He liked to deploy Brahim Hemdani just in front of the defence as an insurance policy. That meant just one striker. With their strength and pace, Cousin and Darcheville would always be ahead of me in the pecking order for that position. I knew I would be benched for most of the games, unless the gaffer wanted to use me in a wide role. As I expected, I was named as a sub for the opener against Stuttgart.

They were a big, strong unit and we had to stay with them during the first half when they tried to impose their game on us. It was pretty tight, but they got a lucky opening goal early in the second half when the striker we had been warned to look out for, Mario Gomez, stuck out a leg and deflected a shot into the net. Rather than let the heads go down, we just got stuck in.

Barry Ferguson was awesome, and showed everyone why the Champions League was an arena made for someone like him who is never scared to take the ball. Charlie Adam swerved in a superb equaliser and Ibrox was rocking. Alan Hutton – who was also outstanding – got decked for a clear penalty that Darche scored. We turned the game on its head from 1-0 down to win. There is no doubt that the way we turned that game around gave the team huge confidence. Remember not many of the players had ever contested a Champions

League group game, but we had three points banked and it was the perfect start.

LYON 0 RANGERS 3
2 October 2007

What a night. What a spectacle. And what a feeling to be part of what many people called Rangers' finest European result since the win over Leeds United at Elland Road in 1992. Lyon was a side brimming with quality throughout. They had won six titles on the spin in France and were used to getting into the last sixteen of the Champions League, at the very least, just about every season. But we left the Stade Gerland with all three points after scoring three superb goals.

We knew they would put us under all sorts of pressure. The gaffer reminded everyone beforehand about the need to defend as a team, to make sure we didn't give away cheap free-kicks within forty yards of goal – as their star Brazilian Juninho would have a pop from that distance! He did on a few occasions, but found Allan McGregor in outstanding form. In fact, our whole defence was awesome.

Our only real attack in the first half brought a goal, Lee McCulloch getting on the end of a corner to bullet a header into the net. I don't think Lyon could believe it. It was as if we had no right to score against them. But we hit them with two sucker punches in the second half through Cousin and Beasley and it was amazing looking up at the scoreboard. Lyon 0 Rangers 3. I don't think anyone would have believed it. I came on in the second half as we tried to see the game out, and we did just that to bank six from six in the first two group games.

RANGERS 0 BARCELONA 0
23 October 2007

I was desperate to start this game against Barca and when the manager gave me the nod I was really chuffed. For a Spaniard it meant everything to be playing against them. There was huge interest in the match and I was bombarded for tickets from people here and also in Spain. With six points in the bag we had nothing to lose.

With Lionel Messi, Thierry Henry, Ronaldinho and all the rest in the team, we knew it would be some shift. I have to say that match was probably the hardest I have run without ever seeing the ball. They swarmed all over us and it was pretty miraculous that we didn't lose a goal. Again, Allan and the defence were solid, we rode our luck, but we got a point.

I knew we would take some stick for the way we had lined up, but opening up against Barcelona would have been suicide. Messi accused us afterwards of playing 'anti-football' but what were we supposed to do? Give them all the space in the world to destroy us the way they had been battering teams every week in La Liga? It was an excellent result for us.

BARCELONA 2 RANGERS 0
7 November 2007

For any Spaniard, playing in the Nou Camp is a dream come true. That stadium, and the Bernabeau where Madrid play, are the two cathedrals of football in my country. The match was Rangers' first trip back to Barcelona since 1972 when the club had won the Cup Winners' Cup. On the flight over all the players from that team were invited and it was great to spend time chatting to so many legends that had been part of the club's finest hour.

I had read in the papers before the game that we would have more than 20,000 fans in the city. Some press guys called me for interviews and asked about the travelling numbers, and said they doubted whether the figures would be accurate. 'Wait and see,' I said to them.

Sure enough, there were more than 20,000 fans in the city and it was amazing travelling to the Nou Camp to see Rangers fans all over the place. I was again on the bench as we went with the tried and trusted 4-5-1. To be fair, they just had too much for us that night and won the game quite comfortably. It was 2-0 going on a few more. The one regret I have is that, towards the end after I came on, I blasted in a shot that I thought was a goal from the minute it left my boot. But Victor Valdes made a top save. I was raging. It would have been great to have had a Nou Camp goal.

STUTTGART 3 RANGERS 2
27 November 2007
I was ruled out of this game after dislocating my shoulder, an injury that would rule me out for six weeks which was a nightmare. After taking seven points from the first three matches, we had been in a superb position. Most observers had us already in the knockout stages, which would have been an incredible achievement given the teams in the section. But the gaffer kept stressing that, with the quality we were up against, they would come blasting back at us and we would have to fight really hard to get more points.

For me, we should have won that night in Stuttgart. Charlie Adam put us in front and, even though they went 2-1 up, we were playing very well and deserved to get an equaliser through Barry. But they scored again late on and it would all come down to Lyon at home.

RANGERS 0 LYON 3
12 December 2007

One of the biggest disappointments of my career – and made even worse by the fact I was injured and in the stand to share the pain with the fans. We needed a draw to make it into the last sixteen, but it was win or bust for them. We were nervy from the start and Sidney Govou put them ahead. I just never got the feeling we believed in ourselves enough. But with about ten minutes left, Barry danced his way into the box, showing amazing skill to reach the byline. He squared the ball for Darcheville but, from two yards out, he scooped his effort over the bar.

It was one of those moments that he'll never forget. Inside five minutes we were buried. Karim Benzema, who had shown just why he was rated so highly, scored twice as we pushed forward and the dream was over. The dressing room was like a morgue after that game. In our last three matches we had not taken a point. We had collapsed and gone out. It was very hard to take.

UEFA CUP ROUND OF 32
RANGERS 0 PANATHINAIKOS 0
13 February 2008

It was a long two months before we would return to the European stage against the Greeks. When the draw was made back in December there was little excitement as we were still nursing the hangover of what had happened at home to Lyon. I didn't know much about Panathinaikos but Greek sides, albeit they could blow hot and cold, were always capable. The home leg against them was very dour to be honest, we didn't create enough and they were content to sit for the draw. It left the odds stacked against us for Athens.

PANATHINAIKOS 1 RANGERS 1
21 February 2008

The game that kick-started our run! We made a shoddy start to the match and as we drifted along at 1-0 down I don't think many people expected us to turn the tie around. It was as if we were happy just to let the UEFA Cup adventure end before it had even begun, which was simply not good enough – and the manager let us know about it at half time.

We gradually grew into the game and started to make some half chances. Then, with seven minutes or so left, a cross came in and the ball bobbled around before landing at my feet. I just took one hit and smashed it into the net. 1-1. We held on and went through on away goals. It was one of the most important goals I had ever scored, both in terms of keeping us alive in the competition, and sending us off on what would be an amazing journey . . .

UEFA CUP ROUND OF 16
RANGERS 2 WERDER BREMEN 0
6 March 2008
Looking back, I would say that night was one of the best performances of our mammoth European run. Bremen were a top side with a host of star men in their team. They were better than Stuttgart, whom we had faced in the Champions League, by some distance. I don't think anyone gave us a chance. But we set-up well against them at Ibrox, again with the 4-5-1.

I used to laugh at people giving us, and the manager, stick for the tactics we used. It was getting us results. Was that not supposed to be the name of the game? Just before the end of a high tempo first half, big Cousin hit a speculative shot from about forty yards. It was an effort their keeper should have dealt with but he fumbled the ball and it shot up into the air and then bounced down over the line. 1-0. Bremen were rattled. When Steven Davis knocked home the second we had them all over the place and really should have killed off the tie. But it gave us the perfect platform for Germany and what we hoped would be the night that took us into the quarter-finals.

WERDER BREMEN 1 RANGERS 0
13 March 2008
We had major injury and suspension problems for the second leg in Germany. The gaffer took me aside and said I would be starting up front on my own – against two six-foot-five plus defenders in Naldo and Mertesacker! It was like being in the land of giants when the game started and I moved up front to be confronted by these two enormous figures.

Bremen went for us right from the start. It was one-way traffic but our defence was again in top form and Allan McGregor had the game of his life. I had a hell of a shift up front. The ball would get punted up from the back and I knew I had to make a nuisance of myself to try and give the lads at the back at a bit of a breather, but with the size of the guys I was up against, there was nothing I could do! Allan made a stunning save from Sanogo as they hit us with everything they had but we held on to make it through. It was an amazing feeling at the end, and for the first time I'd say we did start to believe that we might have had a chance of going all the way.

UEFA CUP QUARTER FINALS
RANGERS 0 SPORTING LISBON 0
3 April 2008
There was massive tension in the air when we faced Sporting at home. It was hard for us as we had all the first leg matches at home, which does make it hard to strike a balance. You want to go forward and try to score, but you also want to avoid losing an away goal. If you have the second match at home, you know exactly what you must do in order to get through. I think that factor again choked the game for us. There were few opportunities created, but even though we had not managed to get a lead to take to Portugal, we were confident enough that, after our away results in the campaign, we could go there and do the business again.

SPORTING LISBON 0 RANGERS 2
10 April 2008

The night we started to dream! Alongside Bremen at home, the performance in Lisbon – especially the second half – ranks as the best we played. They were a good side, although I didn't think they were on the same level as the Germans we had beaten in the round before. I looked around the dressing room before the game and wondered how much more the players could give. We were being submerged in fixtures, the numbers were reducing all the time with injuries, but we were now within touching distance of a semi-final spot.

After an opening period when we had to hold on a bit, we came to life. The passing, the movement, the ability to counter attack. Darcheville's first goal was as classic a counter-attacking goal as you'll ever see and Steven Whittaker's solo effort was fantastic. The scenes on the pitch at the end were really emotional. No one had given us a chance of getting to this stage. But we had rammed all the critics and snipers words back down their throats.

UEFA CUP SEMI-FINALS
RANGERS 0 FIORENTINA 0
24 April 2008

I had major butterflies in my stomach when the boss told me I was starting against the Italians. It was uncanny that the draw had us again playing at home in the first match. The game was to follow a pretty familiar script as we dug in, kept our shape, and didn't do too much at the other end.

We knew that if we kept a clean sheet, we would be in with a chance as that had served us well in Athens, Bremen and

Lisbon. Fiorentina were a classy outfit, they had the better of the few opportunities created, but again it was a night when I think the sense of what was on the line, how close we were to the final in Manchester, maybe took too much of a grip on us and was reflected in the performance.

FIORENTINA 0 RANGERS 0
1 May 2008

An evening that will live with me to the day I die. One of the weird things about the build-up to that game was how calm we were. I don't know if all the nerves had been used up, or if there were just realism in the squad that we knew what it would take having come through so much together. The Italians didn't lose many games on their own turf and they were big favourites to see us off. But the gaffer and the management team were brilliant. They would pull players aside at the hotel for little chats, get everyone together and tell us we had come so far, now go and take the final step.

In the end, after everything that had been written and spoken prior to the second leg, I think we just wanted to get out there. I was on the bench again, which I expected. The 4-5-1 would again have to see us home, we hoped, and it would take a massive performance from every player.

Neil Alexander had come into the team as keeper after Allan McGregor had injured his knee and ankle. I felt for Greegsy as he had played such a huge part in getting us to the semi-final stage, but he would have to sit it out. Neil, though, in the couple of matches he had played, had shown he was a more than able deputy.

I got the feeling that night that Fiorentina just kept thinking the goal would come. They probed and pressed without ever putting us under the pressure we had endured in Bremen, for example. The longer the match went on at 0-0, the more it suited us. With ten minutes to go, I was thrown on in place of Steven Davis and we headed into extra time. Fiorentina started to up the pace and go after the one goal it looked as though it would take to settle this tie. Then big Daniel Cousin got sent off for a crazy incident down in the corner.

He was already on a yellow card when he got pulled up for a soft foul. He went head to head with their defender who went down as though he had been head-butted, and Dan was sent packing. We had ten minutes of extra time to see out with a man down. But we held on like our lives depended on it.

Into penalty kicks. The tension and drama on that pitch was incredible. Right now I still get goosebumps thinking about it. Ally McCoist and Kenny McDowall went around taking the names of the penalty takers. I put myself down as number five. I had taken some big spot kicks in matches like Old Firm games and was confident enough that I could deal with it. When Barry Ferguson missed, and they scored their first one, it didn't look good. I could see the pain on Barry's face as he trudged back to the halfway line where we were all standing, linked with our arms around the shoulder of the next man. We tried to console him. He was Mr Rangers. It could happen to anyone, we said. But he was gutted.

They held the advantage, but Steven Whittaker and Sasa Papac scored to make it 2-2. Neil Alexander then made a superb save from Liverani and Brahim Hemdani rammed home his effort to put us 3-2 up. You could have cut the tension with a knife as we stood way back on the halfway line watching what was going on.

Over to the left I could see the Rangers fans banked in their section. What must be going through their minds I thought to myself? Christian Vieri was a striker who had once ruled Italy. He was on the way down in terms of his career, but I fully expected him to score his penalty and make it 3-3. What happened next left us all stunned. He took a few steps, lent back too much and ballooned his effort over the bar. We just exploded. It was 3-2. We had one penalty taker left from the original list of five, the man who would have the chance to send Rangers to Manchester. It was my time.

I just put my head down and stared at the grass below me as I walked up to the penalty box. Behind me I could hear some of the lads shouting encouragement, but I tried to retain my focus and just blank everything out. It was me against Sebastian Frey. I always made my mind up about which way I would hit the ball on penalties. Some players just make the call as they run up, but I knew I would hit it to Frey's left, as close to the corner as I could. I spotted the ball, took a deep breath and stepped back. There were all sorts of thoughts going through my head. The goal against Red Star way way back that had started the European run. The goal in Athens. Maybe it was destiny that it had all come down to me.

I started my run, opened up my right foot and struck the ball perfectly. Frey went the other way and the ball flew into the net. What a feeling of unbridled joy. I raced over to the Rangers fans and slid onto my knees.

The look on the faces of the fans at the front will live with me forever. The next thing I was under a sea of bodies as my teammates made it from the centre-circle to join me. The scenes were just incredible as we embraced. The gaffer gave me a huge bear hug. He was lost for words. We all were a bit, I think. Back in the dressing room we just tried to take stock of what we had achieved. We were into the UEFA Cup Final. The first Rangers team to reach a European final since 1972. The scenes at the airport were amazing. The fans mobbed me. I was lifted and bounced around. Sheer chaos. Utter delirium. Florence will live with me forever.

UEFA CUP FINAL: MANCHESTER
Zenit St Petersburg 2 Rangers 0
14 May 2008

In our last game before Manchester I scored twice against Dundee United and played as well as I had for some time. I hoped that would maybe lead to me getting a start against the Russians. Everyone wanted to be involved. It was the club's biggest game for thirty-six years. It was really exciting being involved in all of the build up to the game. The demand for tickets was crazy, as you would expect. We had the media open day, all the preparations in terms of when we would be going down. I knew that Rangers would take tens of thousands of fans, as the game would only be three hours drive away from Glasgow. But the numbers that eventually did make the trip were way beyond anything that anyone had predicted.

In training before the match at the City of Manchester Stadium I wondered if the gaffer would change from the 4-5-1 system that had got us to the final. I thought that, if he wanted to be more attack minded even in that system, I might have started in the wide left role that would come down to either myself or Steven Whittaker, depending on what the gaffer opted for. When the team was named, Steven started and I was named as a sub. I was gutted; anyone who doesn't start a cup final is always disappointed. I felt I had maybe earned a starting slot, but you always have to respect the manager's call and he had masterminded things well to this stage.

It was always going to be a different challenge for us against the Russians as there was no home and away leg. One game. Winner takes all. We had set up all along to keep things tight at the back, spring onto the break to try and get goals, but there would be no return leg to salvage things. We had to find the balance between keeping the back door bolted and offering a threat. Dick Advocaat, the former Rangers boss, managed Zenit, of course. Listening to what he said before the game, I honestly believe Dick would have rather been playing any other team in the final than us. Why? He would have wanted Rangers to win the UEFA Cup, if it had been against anyone but the team he managed.

I could tell the Russians fancied it against us. They were billed as dark horses, but from the videos we watched it was obvious they could play. They had great technique, pace and some top players. It would need something very special from us, given that the hectic schedule of games we had to undertake was unquestionably taking its toll. But we were capable of something special. Our results en-route to Manchester were evidence of that.

The first half of the game was pretty even. We had one or two half chances, but I felt we looked jaded. The lads looked as though there wasn't a lot left in the tank. It was our nineteenth European game of the season – effectively half an SPL campaign on top of the one we had to cope with – and Zenit started to take a grip after the break. When they scored with just under twenty minutes left, it was to be a defining moment. We didn't have enough energy to lift it and, as much as there was no shortage of effort, as there never was, we lacked any kind of cutting edge against such a professional outfit. I was pitched on in place of Sasa Papac with thirteen minutes to go, but there was little time to get into things. They picked us off to win 2-0 and it all ended in a bit of a whimper.

I think the one over-riding regret for me was that, apart from not starting the game, we didn't make a better fist of the final. There is no doubt in my mind that if a fully fit, fresh Rangers team had met Zenit, we would have made a far bigger impression on the game – but we were dead on our feet and ran out of steam at the very last hurdle.

The players were too dejected afterwards to be made fully aware of the fact that there had been some crowd problems in the city. That was a huge disappointment as the vast majority of our fans had been superb and had been at every game, every step of the way. I wish Manchester could have turned out differently. You never say never in football, but it's likely to be the one and only European final I am involved in.

That said, the memories of that 2007/08 European campaign will live long in my mind. It had everything and I was proud to have played my part.

PAIN AND ANGER

The message was plain and simple from Walter Smith as he embarked on his first full season in charge at Rangers: 'Let's get the SPL title back!'

Some ten months on from that declaration of intent, after we had given our all and then some, we would end up falling just short of delivering to the boss what he had asked for. Instead of the championship medal that we deserved, we were left nursing plenty of anger and frustration at the way the fixture list was allowed to pan out and cost us glory in the domestic prize that mattered most.

Celtic had almost strolled to two-in-a-row without us mustering any kind of genuine challenge; both previous league seasons had more or less been over for Rangers by Christmas and that was just completely unacceptable at a club with our tradition and history.

Walter Smith had guided Rangers to nine-in-a-row during his first spell as manager. There was no doubting his CV on that front. He knew how to win league championships. I hoped that would rub off on all of us.

Everything the manager had done after picking up the pieces of the Le Guen shambles had been a success. You could see the road-plan he had in his mind beginning to be mapped out in theory: make us hard to beat; finish second in the league; get some respectability back to the club. Since his arrival in January 2007, that had all been achieved. We had finished the second half of the league season strongly, beating Celtic twice. He had the complete respect of every player, but I always knew he would get to work on building his own team, one he hoped would sustain a challenge.

I hoped that I had done enough, shown him that I had something to offer, to make sure that I got to stay. I had a good feeling about what Walter Smith was going to do and I wanted to be a part of it.

Life at the club had been a roller coaster for me in the three seasons up until the start of the 2007/08 campaign; a championship medal in my first, then two seasons of turmoil which had seen me work under three different managers. I just knew right away that things would be different under Walter Smith. I wanted to be a part of his new-look squad; be part of the mission to try and wrestle the title back across the city from Celtic.

Two old warriors had left the club; Stefan Klos and Dado Prso. They had been magnificent servants to Rangers and would be sadly missed. Walter Smith also cleared out more or less all of the remnants from the ill-fated Le Guen tenure. Libor Sionko and Jose Pierre-Fanfan moved on, while Filip Sebo was also shipped out on loan.

Le Guen's big mistake, as I have already said, was signing the wrong kind of players for the SPL. I didn't think for one minute that Walter Smith would make the same errors, not with his experience of the Scottish game. Le Guen had also not spent much money the summer before, maybe around

£4million. That surprised a lot of people as it was widely claimed he would have a big budget for new players. But Rangers quickly started to get active in the transfer market prior to the 2007/08 season, before our amazing European run.

In had come three players on Bosmans – Jean Claude Darcheville from Bordeaux, Alan Gow from Falkirk and Kirk Broadfoot from St Mirren. The latter two were young, hungry guys who had done well at their clubs. They were also Rangers fans. I felt they would be solid additions.

DaMarcus Beasley, an American winger, was snapped up from PSV Eindhoven. I didn't know too much about him, but he had been on loan at Manchester City and looked quick and direct. Two major investments went on Lee McCulloch, the Scotland internationalist who came in from Wigan for around £2.3m, and Carlos Cuellar, a countryman from Spain who arrived for around the same fee as big Lee.

I knew Cuellar from the games against Osasuna in the UEFA Cup just a few months previously. I also did some check calls to people I knew in Spain and right away they said this guy would be outstanding for us. He was big, strong and quick. But he was also a real winner. I liked the idea that another Spanish player would be there with me at Rangers.

After a tough pre-season in Germany which was geared towards the start of the Champions League qualifiers and the big SPL kick-off, we returned for glamour friendly matches at home to Ajax and Chelsea. There was a real sense of antic-ipation about the new campaign and the fans, I sensed, were optimistic that we could really achieve something.

First up was Ajax. Carlos Cuellar was already proving to be a huge hit, on and off the pitch. I struck up a strong friendship with him right away. I tried to help him settle into Glasgow, to find a house and just assist him as much as possible. On the field he was beginning to show why the boss wanted him. He impressed everyone and scored a goal on his home debut against Ajax as we drew 1-1.

The following Saturday we faced Jose Mourinho's Chelsea superstars. Now some of these pre-season matches can be pretty mind-numbing affairs. They are often played without an edge and there are loads of substitutions as managers focus more on getting match fitness and the fans don't really get to see a genuine contest. But the Chelsea game was something else. The match was a 50,000 sell-out at Ibrox and the atmosphere was like a Champions League night!

Both sides went at it to win the game and with five minutes to go I opened the scoring. The place was going mad. It was a long time since I had seen anything like that from our fans. It was a sign they were getting up for the new campaign. We won the match 2-0 and even the Chelsea players said it was the best pre-season atmosphere they had ever sampled!

We started our SPL challenge at Inverness on 4 August. By this time the manager had again been busy in the market, signing Steven Whittaker from Hibs for £2m and also bringing in Daniel Cousin from Lens for £1m. They were both excellent additions, I felt. With Darcheville and Cousin signed – both centre forwards – and Kris Boyd also there – I had a feeling early on that I would be used more in the wide roles by the manager. As I have said, that was never my favoured position but he had built such a strong squad we were all just going to have to fight it out.

I knew any opportunity I had, simply had to be taken. I worked as hard as I ever had in training to get my strength and fitness to maximum levels. And that paid off on the opening day up at Inverness, never an easy venue. I managed to rifle home a shot from just outside the box as we ran out 3-0 winners. It was the perfect start to the league season for us. That was crucial. In the two previous seasons we had dropped daft points and allowed Celtic to get ahead early on. On the evidence of their successes under Strachan, it was clear they would not drop much. If we wanted to sustain a challenge, then consistency would be the key. That certainly proved to be the case in the first month of the season.

We defeated St Mirren, Falkirk, Kilmarnock and Gretna to make it five wins from five. On the final day of August, one of the longest running transfer sagas I'd ever seen ended when we signed Steven Naismith from Kilmarnock for around £2m. It was more competition in the forward areas, but he was a fine young talent. I knew I would have to just knuckle down and fight it out with the rest.

I'll admit it was frustrating for me as I did struggle to get a starting jersey. It was around about this time that I started being referred to as an 'impact player', something that has kind of stuck with me now.

The assumption in that description is that I am better used coming on when the team needs something to happen, rather than being a player who could start matches. I have never agreed with that, naturally. It is difficult to pick up the pace of a game when you are just getting thrown on for twenty minutes here and there. You also struggle to stay 'match sharp'. I wanted to start more matches, but it was the manager's call.

As we moved into the autumn, the team was doing well in the league and we were matching Celtic all the way. Hibs had also started the season in good form. As always, the first

Old Firm meeting of the season would be very important. I was given the nod to start by the manager for the first game at Ibrox in October. Like any time we faced Celtic, I was fired up, absolutely aware of how important it was to give everything for my team and for the fans. If we could win this game, it would show we meant business in the title. Sure, we had won the last two meetings of the season before – but it had meant nothing more than pride as Celtic had things wrapped up. This time it was about points. Vital points at that.

I started on the left of a midfield four, with the instruction to try and get at the Celtic back line as much as I could, but also to ensure I didn't forget the defensive side of my shift.

Just before the half-hour mark of a fairly even Old Firm clash, Alan Hutton swung over a dangerous ball from the right. I gambled that the pace on his cross would carry it past the two central defenders, Stephen McManus and Gary Caldwell. It did. I stooped low and sent in a header that squeezed past Artur Boruc into the corner of the net. 1-0 Rangers.

It was an amazing feeling, like any goal against Celtic. More importantly, it gave us the lead and the platform to play. We bossed the game from there and Barry Ferguson then put us 2-0 up in the second half. Towards the end, Evander Sno decked Charlie Adam in the box. It was a clear penalty. Like I'd done before, I grabbed the ball right away. I felt I had played well in the game and my confidence was high. I sent the kick past Boruc. We ran out 3-0 winners in the most comfortable Old Firm victory I had been involved in.

It had been a good day for Rangers as the win had taken us level on twenty-two points with our city rivals after ten league matches. And it had been a good day for me. As I sat at home that night, I reflected on scoring two goals, and also the fact that I might be able to use that double as a launch pad for more starting berths. The season was getting busier and busier with matches in all different competitions and I knew that the gaffer would need everyone. But then, disaster struck.

I played in a bounce game against Middlesbrough at Murray Park. It was a pretty low key affair and was designed for players who were not featuring very often to stay match sharp. In the first half I tried to dart between two of their defenders, big lads, and I went flying. As I landed, I felt a searing pain in my left shoulder. I knew right away it was serious. I went straight to hospital for an MRI scan. My worst fears were confirmed. I had dislocated it, quite badly. The only cure would be rest. I would be out for at least two months, the doctors said.

That period of inactivity did, however, allow me to sort out one piece of crucial business – my future. The club had made it known to my agent, Jorge, and myself that they would be keen for me to sign a new deal, as my current contract was set to expire in the summer of 2008.

There was a fair bit of interest in me from clubs, mostly in Spain, as is the case when it's known you are into the final six months of your existing agreement. But I wanted to stay. There was no real question of going anywhere else in my mind. I told Jorge that, and asked him to strike a deal with Martin Bain. A two-year extension, until the summer of 2010, was agreed. That meant I would be looking at six years at Rangers, something that really pleased me.

I also had the security of knowing where I would be for the next couple of years and the contract would take me up until I was thirty-one years old. Deep down it was a nice feeling to know that the manager wanted to keep me, as he had moved a lot of players on after coming in to take over from Le Guen.

In total, the shoulder injury caused me to miss eight matches. I returned as a substitute on 5 January against Dundee United, a game that we won 2-0. The winter months had been good for us and we had moved to the top of the table, piling the pressure on Celtic.

The teams were supposed to meet in the traditional Ne'erday match on 2 January at Parkhead but the game was postponed after the tragic death of Motherwell's Phil O'Donnell. It was heart-breaking to see his wife and kids going to Fir Park and looking at all the floral tributes that had been left. Barry Ferguson, Lee McCulloch and some of the other guys at our club who knew Phil had gone to the tribute as well to pay their respects. He had collapsed on the pitch in a game against Dundee United on 29 December and died. It left the whole of the game stunned.

I knew it would be a huge struggle for me to get back into the gaffer's starting plans after the injury setback. I came off the bench in the next six games, including the 2-0 win over Hearts in the Co-operative Insurance League Cup semi-final that booked our place in the first final of the season.

It was a weird feeling that night at Hampden. The place was half empty, the weather was dreadful and there was a bit of depression in the air amongst our support after the dramatic late events in the January transfer window.

Alan Hutton had been flying. In fact, he was as good as any full back in the UK at that time, his performances for the national team and also for us in the Champions League earning him a lot of admirers. Spurs had come in with a mammoth £8m offer for him very early in the window, but he had not chosen to go. I understood how Alan was feeling as being born and bred a Rangers fan it was a huge decision for him.

The money Spurs had offered was too good to turn down. He was also being offered a contract that would have changed his life forever. Alan never said much as the month of January had progressed, but it was clearly weighing on his mind. His performances remained at their usual high standards, but you could see he was being torn. It must have been hard for him to decide whether or not to leave Rangers, the club he loved, for the English Premiership were he would earn a lot of money but have to fight hard to get regular football, which he was enjoying with us. Then, just a couple of days before the window closed, he opted to leave.

I came in to Murray Park as usual for training and the word quickly spread that Alan had come in the night before, got his stuff and was now on his way to London to sign for Spurs. It was a huge blow for us. We were still in the UEFA Cup, we were clear of Celtic at the top of the league and we were into the first cup final of the season. But we had just sold our best and most consistent player from the first half of the season.

The fans were really upset and I think they wanted some of the money to be spent right away. Steven Davis came in on loan from Fulham; Neil Alexander had arrived from Ipswich to replace Roy Carroll, who had left, while Christian Dailly also arrived after Ugo Ehiogu moved on. We had brought in good experience and top quality in Steven Davis. But how would the loss of Hutton affect us?

The month of February, for me, was the first real sign of what lay in store in terms of our fixture congestion. We had seven games in the shortest month of the year. Effectively, we were playing a game every four days. Now we had a decent enough squad in terms of numbers, but it was clearly going to be a huge task to stay alive in all competitions. The press quickly latched on to things and questioned whether or not we could pull off an amazing 'quadruple'.

The manager and the backroom team did everything they could to keep us fresh. We prepared properly for matches, had as much rest given to us as we could afford, and the training sessions were designed to more or less just keep us ticking over. The demand was incredible, but we were meeting every challenge head on. Domestically, I hadn't scored a goal since October and it was eating away at me. The fact I was also being named as a sub almost every game was frustrating, but I tried to see it from the manager's point of view as well.

Players are never happy when they don't start, but the gaffer always kept my spirits up by talking to me about his decisions when I asked him. There was no problem between us at all and I just kept trying to give my all when he called on me. At the end of February we faced Hearts at Tynecastle. It was always a tough venue to get points. We battered them 4-0 and I scored twice after coming off the bench. We were determined not to let the schedule bring us down and that performance sent out the message we wanted.

I have to admit it was actually quite difficult keeping track of what competition we were playing in as the games came thick and fast! We faced Hibs at Ibrox in a Scottish Cup replay on 9 March after drawing 0-0 at Easter Road – back on 3 February. To highlight the chaos that was going on, it was the first free date we had to play them again – and we had played eight matches in between the first game and the replay!

The gaffer sent me on as a sub with twenty minutes to go. We were 1-0 up after a superb Chris Burke goal, but Hibs were beginning to come more and more into the game as the affect of so many matches started to take its toll on our legs. It had been a fiery match, as games against Hibs often are.

With ten minutes to go I dived into a tackle with their defender, Thierry Gattueshi right in front of the technical areas. He was a big lad and I saw him come flying in towards me. It was just one of those things, I tried to be as strong in the tackle as I could but the way I jumped forward both feet came off the ground and caught him as he got to the ball first. It wasn't the best tackle in the world, I have to be honest, although there was never any intention to hurt him.

As I hauled myself off the ground, I could see the Hibs manager Mixu Paatelainen going mental. He was screaming for a red card. He didn't need to tell Craig Thomson, the ref. The card was already out. I was off. As I trudged up the tunnel it was mayhem. Walter Smith had raced from the Rangers dugout and squared up to Paatelainen. He was raging at the way he had reacted and all hell broke loose. The gaffer was sent to the stand for the closing stages. I think he did it to provoke a reaction from the crowd. And it worked.

He knew we were dead on our feet and would have to see the last ten minutes of the match out a man down. If Hibs had equalised, I don't think we would have had the energy for extra time. And the boss knew it. The punters got a head of steam on and dragged the team over the line. In the dressing room, I was gutted. I had let the team down.

But there was worse news to follow. I was sent off for violent conduct. The punishment for that means you automatically miss the next domestic game, no matter the competition. It quickly hit me. I would be out of the League Cup Final against Dundee United the following Sunday.

That night I was devastated, playing the tackle over and over again in my head. I saw it on the TV highlights. It didn't look good. And I had to pay the ultimate price. The next weekend, in one of the best finals for years, we came from behind twice to draw 2-2 with Dundee United after extra time. Kris Boyd scored both goals. We won the Cup on penalties.

I went around with the boys on the victory parade, but it never feels the same in a suit. It was a hard one for me to take. I should have been there to help the team, and to enjoy the moment. Don't get me wrong; it was brilliant to win the trophy and to bank the first piece of silverware. In fact, it was pretty miraculous that we managed to come back against United, as our preparation for the final had been an energy sapping ninety minutes in Bremen on the Thursday night in the UEFA Cup! The spirit the boys showed that day was amazing. But I could see cracks appearing. I feared for us in the run in, especially as we were getting no breathing space.

We were left to fight on three fronts now; the SPL, the Scottish Cup and Europe. The cancellation of the Old Firm game at Parkhead in January had led to a situation where there was just no suitable date to play it before Celtic were scheduled back at Ibrox on 29 March. Effectively, we would then be playing them twice at Ibrox in succession, after the earlier game in October, and then we would have back-to-back games at Parkhead.

We knew the home game would be absolutely crucial. We had a small lead at the top of the table. If we could win that one, it would increase the gap and give us some breathing space in what was now a crazy schedule of games. The Old Firm game at the end of March was our eighth match in thirty days. With so much at stake, it was a bit of a battle and not as open as some of the more recent encounters between the sides. Kevin Thomson slid home the only goal in the first half and we held on to win 1-0. When the dust settled we were six points clear with a game in hand. There were nine matches left. People said it was all over. We knew it never was. Not with the games we had to cram in.

It was around this time that the SPL hierarchy started to realise that there could be genuine chaos on the horizon. If we kept going in Europe, and with the way we were storming on in the Scottish Cup as well – into the last eight against Partick Thistle – then there was just not going to be enough room to fit in all of Rangers' games.

As you would expect, everyone started working to their own agendas. There is no love for Rangers in Scotland, despite what some people seem to think, and when the first mention came of the season possibly being extended, it was roundly shot down. It actually became the real hot topic just about every day in the press and the radio phone-ins as we progressed further in the UEFA Cup and the problems that the administrators could face became clearer and clearer.

As players, there was nothing we could do about the situation. We had to try and get on with playing and let our chairman, chief executive and manager deal with all the politics.

By the middle of April, the doomsday scenario that the SPL wanted to avoid was beginning to come to fruition. We had beaten Sporting Lisbon to make it into the semi-finals of the UEFA Cup, wiping out another two midweeks in the run-in, which had been set aside for the outstanding league games we still had to play. We were also into the semi-finals of the Scottish Cup against St Johnstone – that meant a weekend would also be taken out of the equation.

We were scheduled to play Celtic at Parkhead in the first of our double headers that would have a huge bearing on where the title would end up. There was a major edge to that game. Celtic had made it clear they were not in favour of the season being extended, should we be unable to cram all our matches in.

That did not come as a major surprise! They were our rivals; they didn't want us to get an inch. We were even told they had lined up a tour to Japan at the end of the season that meant they could not play on beyond the designated league season end date of 18 May. I am still waiting for them to go on that tour!

Of course, pressure was applied from both sides onto the SPL. That is where they should have been strong and did what they felt was right. Not be bullied. There were all sorts going on behind the scenes, I have been told, but we knew if we had taken care of business against Celtic we would have had one hand on the title. We were seven points clear going into the game.

It was, as you can imagine with the stakes so high, a real battle. The tackles were flying in and the referee, Kenny Clark, struggled to keep a lid on what was happening. Celtic went ahead with a screamer of a goal from Shunsuke Nakamura. He hit a shot from over thirty yards that swerved and dipped past Allan McGregor into the net.

I was on the bench and, as was so often the case, the gaffer threw me on at half time to try and get us a goal. I played on the right hand side of midfield, pushing forward to try and get into attack. When a long ball was sent down the channel in the second half, I managed to get in behind the Celtic defence. Head down I drove into their box. The ball set up perfectly for me. I hit across it. Low and hard was my aim. It flew past Artur Boruc into the right hand corner of the net. It was the best Old Firm goal I had scored. 1-1. A result that, given the circumstances, would do us fine. Celtic were desperate. They had to win. We just had to hold on.

In one passage of play, I gathered the ball in midfield and burst forward. As I was running clear, I was chopped down from behind by a two-footed lunge from Jan Vennegoor of Hesselink. To me it was a straight red card offence. The back of my leg was in agony. There was no attempt to play the ball as it was a yard in front of me and he had dived in from directly behind me. But Clark only showed him a yellow card. I thought that was a very, very poor decision. And it was one that would have a huge bearing later on.

I felt we were comfortable in the game. But then, as often happens in Old Firm games, crazy things can happen. Nakamura cut inside over on the left hand side of the box. He curled in another shot that was goal-bound and had beaten Allan all hands up. But Carlos Cuellar – our rock at the back – jumped up on the goal line and deliberately punched the ball over the bar. Straight red card. Penalty to Celtic. It seemed as though things had swung their way. But Allan pulled off a superb save from Scott McDonald and we were still level. He also injured his knee in the process and, when he limped off to be replaced by Neil Alexander, it looked as though the fates were really against us.

I thought we had seen the game out. As I stared up at the

giant Parkhead scoreboard we were deep into injury time. But in Old Firm games you can never believe you are there until the whistle sounds. A deep cross from the right. A header across goal. And bang. With seconds left, Hesselink stooped in to score. He should not even have been on the pitch after his tackle on me. But he was. And he had struck the killer blow.

Seconds later the final whistle blew. Now, Aiden McGeady and myself have never been close, shall we say. He doesn't like me and I don't have much time for him. He is a fantastic player, but our swords have crossed a few times. When the game was 1-1, I had been given a bit of stick from the Celtic fans in the Main Stand after making a tackle on him. I gestured as though he was in my pocket by patting the back of my shorts as if there was a pocket there! That went down well.

At the final whistle, after Celtic had snatched a 2-1 win, he raced past me and let's just say enjoyed the moment. I was raging at the way we had just lost the game and we squared up. Players from both sides raced in and there was an almighty melee. That can happen in Old Firm games, passions can run high.

There was a lot of shoving and pushing as the ref and his assistants waded in. When we got back to the dressing room, Davie Weir was called out. He was taken to the ref's room and red carded for his part in the bust-up. Celtic's Gary Caldwell suffered the same fate. Just another Old Firm game.

The significance of that night, however, was that it gave Celtic hope. Had we held on for just a minute longer I think they would have felt it was all over.

The way the fixtures had panned out after the split, our next league game was back at Parkhead eleven days later. We had played Fiorentina at Ibrox on the Thursday night in the first leg of our UEFA Cup semi-final – hardly ideal preparation, but we got on with it.

By this time, the SPL had announced their plans for the conclusion to the season. There were two fixture scenarios unveiled; one if we got to the final in Manchester, and one if we didn't. If we were to get to the UEFA Cup Final, the league season would be extended by four days!

It was meltdown. Our fans were going crazy, as were the management. Everyone could see we were staggering along under the weight of the congestion. The SFA mooted a plan to put back the Scottish Cup Final – which we had also reached after beating St Johnstone – by a week to 31 May. That would have allowed the SPL more time to fit in our games fairly. For me, that was the option that should have been taken.

People kept using the phrase that it had to be a 'level playing field' but how was it for us? We were penalised by our own league for reaching a European Final. That is the bottom line. I took calls from people in Spain who could not believe what was going on. They said our country was a laughing stock. The games would pan out, if we reached Manchester, in such a way that we would play three games in the space of six days in order for the season to finish on 22 May. The cup final against Queen of the South would go ahead as planned on 24 May.

We returned to Parkhead on 27 April. Again, this was another frenetic battle. Celtic took an early lead when McDonald went through and scored. It was later shown he was offside. We hit back through goals from Davie Weir and Daniel Cousin and we were worth a 2-1 lead going toward half time. Then McDonald struck again to square things up

167

But in the second half, as the legs began to go, Celtic got stronger. We lost Davie Weir to an injury and ended up with Amdy Faye – who had hardly played a game – and Christian Dailly as the centre half pairing. Celtic got a penalty and won the match 3-2. It was another crushing blow for us. But we had to get our heads up for the midweek match, which was the second leg of the UEFA Cup semi-final against Fiorentina in Italy.

I know people would never have said it publicly, but if we had lost that night in Florence it would have made life a lot easier for them. We didn't. And we were forced into the night-mare fixture run-in from our point of view.

After drawing 0-0 at Hibs on the Sunday after Florence, it was neck and neck between Celtic and us. I looked around the dressing room that day and wondered how much more we had to give.

We beat Motherwell 1-0 the following midweek at home. Another row had exploded. Our board asked the SPL if they would postpone our game against Dundee United on the Saturday to give us a free weekend to prepare for the UEFA Cup Final against Zenit in Manchester. It was rejected. I think we always knew it would be. They said there was simply no room for another game to be squeezed in had they agreed. There would have been – had they extended the season properly and knocked the Scottish Cup Final back a week!

I always remember Dick Advocaat, the Zenit boss and former Rangers manager, saying that only in Scotland could that happen to one of the teams. That only in Scotland could self-interest be put ahead of the image of the game, the standing of our league. We were representing Scotland in a UEFA Cup

Final. Not that you would have known that by the decisions that were going on.

We played United. We won the game 3-1 and I scored twice. Our final three games in the league would all be away at Motherwell on 17 May, St Mirren on 19 May and Aberdeen on 22 May. We would then have to meet Queen of the South in the Scottish Cup Final on 24 May. That was less than forty-eight hours after we would kick our final ball in the league. And people still try to tell me that was fair?

We got on with it. A combination of the after-affects of losing in Manchester to the Russians and the fact we were all shattered led to a 1-1 draw at Motherwell that saw Celtic take the initiative in the title race. We would have to go to Paisley on the Monday night and rattle in plenty of goals to be in the box seat going into the final round of matches. Much as we had a real go at it, we could only win 3-0. Under normal circumstances, that would have been an excellent return at a tough venue like Love Street. But these were not normal circumstances. We went into the final night. Rangers at Pittodrie. Celtic seventy-five miles down the road at Tannadice. They were ahead on goal difference. Both teams were level on points and had to win.

Outside of Parkhead, Pittodrie was as hard a place as anywhere to go. They were well pumped up, as usual, to try and wreck things for us. Our players were dead on their feet that night. It was a game we just never looked like winning from pretty early on. Aberdeen scored two quick goals midway through the second half and Celtic had taken the lead at Tannadice. It was all over.

The manager sent me on. I was gutted. Around me I could see the faces of players who had given everything in the longest season in Rangers' history. But things had conspired against us. Essentially, the UEFA Cup run had cost us the league title. We had lost in Manchester. And now we were losing the league. It hurt like hell. In the final few weeks of the season, it felt as though everything was against us.

We just could not find that extra surge to pull ourselves over the line. I lunged into a needless tackle towards the end on Stuart Duff. I looked up and saw another red card over my head from Kenny Clark. As I trudged off, my world had collapsed. Just like the League Cup Final, when I had been sent off in the game before it against Hibs, my dismissal for violent conduct would mean I was suspended for the Scottish Cup Final against Queen of the South. What a nightmare. I couldn't believe what I had done. It was just frustration, hurt, pain and anger all bubbling over and I had made a stupid challenge. We flew home from Aberdeen and I hardly slept a wink.

Whilst Celtic celebrated their title success, three-in-a-row, we had to gather at Murray Park on the Friday and try to prepare for the final. I was out and I was as low as I have ever felt that day. The boys were drained, shattered, but had to go one more time. Despite a scare when Queens got it back to 2-2 after we had been two goals ahead, we won the final 3-2.

It was a muted celebration for us, and our fans. Out of the famous 'quadruple' we had landed the League Cup and the Scottish Cup. But we had missed out on the SPL and the UEFA Cup, the two major ones we wanted. It hurt everyone at the club big time.

To put things into perspective, in the months of April and May of the 2007/08 season we had to play fifteen games in forty-six days. That is just staggering. And major games at that; crucial European ties, Old Firm games, domestic cup semi-finals and finals. What leeway did we get from the SPL? The season was extended by four days.

No matter how things turn out for Rangers in the future, no matter how many league titles are won, what happened that year will always be looked upon with great anger from the players involved, and our fans.

12

NACHO MACNOVO

Scotland is now the place I call home. I have lived here for almost nine years and, in the main, have loved being part of life in this country.

Around eighteen months ago, right out of the blue, I was asked whether I would have played for the Scottish national team; that was certainly an issue that sparked a lengthy debate and led to a meeting between the four home nations – Scotland, England, Wales and Northern Ireland!

Here is the background to what happened, and my honest opinion on what I would have done, had the opportunity actually arisen.

I took a call towards the end of October 2008 from Keith Jackson, one of the sports journalists at the *Daily Record*, a good lad that I have known for a while. Keith explained to me that, due to the fact I had stayed in Scotland for eight years at that time, I was eligible for a British passport. If I followed that through, and gained UK citizenship, then I could be eligible to play for Scotland. George Burley was the national team manager at that team.

I thought at first it was a joke. But the more it was explained to me, the better I understood. I then recalled seeing something on TV about the England manager, Fabio Capello, considering trying to get the Arsenal keeper, Manuel Almunia, to play for them. He had stayed in England long enough to qualify for a passport and so on. I said to Keith that it would be something I would consider, that if the rules were clear and the SFA wanted me, I would see what happened.

Of course the story in the *Record* the next day caused chaos. It set the news agenda for days. Everyone and their granny seemed to have an opinion on whether it was right or wrong, whether a guy born in Spain should be able to play for Scotland. I read with interest what a lot of people had to say.

I had my face put on the body of a player in a Scotland kit; I was called Nacho MacNovo in one headline. In another story they started picking a team from all the other players who had been living in Scotland for over five years and who would be in the same position as me had the rule been agreed. It all became a bit over the top and a bit embarrassing, although there were the usual suspects coming out and saying I wasn't good enough for Scotland and that kind of stuff. As usual, the ones who didn't like you, maybe because you played for Rangers, were having a pop.

The funny thing was that this practice was already happening across world football. There had been several cases of players not born in a particular country actually turning out for them. The outstanding midfielder, Deco, was actually Brazilian born but played for Portugal as he had stayed there and grew up in the country. So it was not unique to me.

Burley had his say on that matter and basically put the issue in the SFA's court. His party line was that if they told him certain players were eligible then he would consider them. There was so much confusion going on that the issue was brought to the top of the agenda at a hastily arranged meeting between the four home nations. They had a gentleman's agreement in place that said they would stick to bloodlines in terms of players who were eligible. It went back as far as grandparents, I believe.

It was announced that they would not consider players under the residency ruling. The door was slammed shut inside a week!

I have been asked the question many times, would I have played for Scotland had it gone the other way? Yes, I would have. I would have had no problem at all pulling on a dark blue jersey if the SFA had chosen to go down another road and the manager wanted me.

I thought long and hard about the issue in the week between the story coming out and the four nations meeting. I viewed it as an opportunity to play international football, to progress as a player. I would have been right up for it and I would have given the team 110 per cent, just the same as I did for Rangers in every game. If the window had opened then why not? Why would I have said no? But, in hindsight, I don't think the four home nations wanted to open the floodgates in terms of players beyond the bloodline ruling.

So that was it. They said they would not use the ruling. Do I think that was right? No. Scotland, Wales and Northern Ireland have gone a fair time without making a major competition. Now I am not saying that I would have made all the difference in trying to achieve that aim. But is it not better for a manager to have as many options open as possible?

And, having played for Rangers for over four years at that time, having played in the Champions League, and having looked at the players in the squad, then I am confident that

I could have done a job for Scotland had they wanted me. Of course, they then tweaked the ruling a bit last year. It was changed to allow players who had been educated in a country for five years to be eligible.

This was the case, or so they thought, with Hearts' Andrew Driver. He had played for England's Under 21 team, but after Craig Levein was appointed he managed to get him to change his mind and commit his senior career to Scotland. It was made public that Driver would turn his back on England and make himself available for Scotland.

But a few weeks later it emerged that he had actually not been educated in Scotland for the required five years. What a farce. I could not believe the boy was left out in the open like that. Surely someone should have had that all checked out before they went public?

With no international prospects at Scotland, I have forged ahead with representing my own 'country'. Not Spain! But Galicia! The Galician national football team is the unofficial side that represents the autonomous community of Galicia in my homeland. They are not recognised by FIFA or UEFA, because the nation overall is represented internationally by the Spanish team. They only ever play friendly games, normally during the winter break in Spain.

They only started playing matches again in 2005 after the team was disbanded in 1930. But the people in the region wanted it to happen and it did.

Since the 1980s there has been a huge public debate on whether or not Galicia should gain full official status, the right to take part in official competitions. This is not only for football, but other sports. In many ways it's like Scotland, Wales or Northern Ireland taking part in competitions when they are all part of the UK. There is not a British team – it's split up into four. Why should Spain not be the same? Galicia and Catalonia could have their own teams. It is a very emotive issue and feelings run high.

I have played for Galicia on two occasions. My first match came against Cameroon in December 2007. The game took place in Vigo, in front of 28,000 fans and we drew 1-1. Michel Salgado, of Real Madrid, was the captain of the Galician side. There are also other top players, such as the Villarreal keeper, Diego Lopez, Ruben from Celtic Vigo and Pablo Alvarez from Deportivo La Coruna who also represent the region. They are all very proud to do so, as am I.

A game was scheduled the following year for 27 December against Iran in La Coruna. It was the same day that we were scheduled to face Celtic at Ibrox, so I informed the officials of the Galician national team that I would be unable to play. I was gutted. But they got back in touch quickly and said they would arrange for a small eight seater private plane to be at Glasgow Airport right after the game to fly me back to Galicia so I could play.

The Old Firm game kicked off at lunchtime and the game in La Coruna was not until 8.45pm so I had time to make it. The plane would then bring me back to Glasgow. My sister, Arantxa, was over for Christmas with us and came with me. It was amazing, we felt like pop-stars being whisked from Ibrox straight to the airport and on to our own private jet! The experience certainly helped me take my mind off the match that we had just lost 1-0 to Celtic.

I played in the game and scored two goals as we beat the Iranians 3-2 in the Riazor Stadium, home of Deportivo La Coruna. The crowd was 12,000. It was another fantastic experience and I hope to play for Galicia as much as I can in the future. It would have been nice to have had an international career with Scotland – maybe I'll just leave that for my son Javier!

13

SINISTER TIMES

The blank envelope that lay on the front doormat in my fiancee's Inverkip flat was to deliver the most chilling threat . . .

There was no name on the front but there was no doubt as to who it was aimed at. The scrawled writing said: 'If you play against Celtic on Sunday, you will get f—— done in. We'll kill you, you Rangers bastard.'

I had to read it a couple of times before it sunk in. It was days before a crucial Old Firm clash at Parkhead on 20 February 2005 and the off-field problems I had encountered since signing for Rangers had just escalated to a whole new level.

I was totally shocked. There had been some unsavoury incidents to deal with in the previous five months or so, but Donna, my fiancee, and I had both tried not to let it bother us. They were just morons, scum, I would say to her. But this was a death threat. I didn't know what to do.

Donna and I sat and discussed whether or not we should bring the police in. My fear was that it was just idiots trying to be big men and if the police had come to see me and had a look at the letter – and it had then leaked to the press which would have been extremely likely – there could have been a huge circus before the game against Celtic. That was the last thing I wanted.

It was the third meeting of the season between the clubs. It was a crucial match in terms of the destination of the SPL title. If it was all over the papers that I had been sent a death threat, then I would have been the centre of attention and I didn't want that. We decided to keep it between us. Looking back, maybe that wasn't the right call. But would they have found the person responsible? Highly unlikely.

I was a bit shaken by the whole thing for a few days. I wasn't living in fear or anything like that, but I was concerned for Donna and the two boys, Dylan and Ross, as she would be in the flat herself over the next few days and I didn't want her to have to put up with any nonsense.

I felt the best option would be to ignore it. And answer these scumbags on the pitch. I was determined to go out and show them that I would not be scared, not be intimidated by anyone or anything. I played at Parkhead that Sunday and scored the second goal as we won 2-0.

There are a number of incidents that have been reported involving me and I want to set the record straight on these. I also want to highlight some of the things that haven't made it into the public domain. The death threat letter came after a succession of incidents in the first season after my move to Rangers from Dundee.

It was funny, when I was at Raith and Dundee you would get the odd bit of banter in the street or out and about from opposition fans, but when I became a Rangers player it moved to a totally different level. It appeared to me that I had become something of a hate figure in the eyes of some of the Celtic fans because I had opted to choose Rangers ahead of their club the summer before.

I have no problem with people not liking me, even when

they don't know me. That is their choice. I play to win, I love Rangers; our fans are what matter to me. But there have been some really disturbing things that I have had to endure as a Rangers player trying to go about my life in Glasgow, without looking for any attention. It's something I have grown used to. I don't like it, but I handle it. I am always aware that I can be targeted. I don't go out much, and when I do, I go with people I know and trust and to places I feel comfortable in. Glasgow can be a fantastic city for an Old Firm player with the passion of the fans, something that not many other places can generate. But it can also be very nasty and leave you wondering where these morons get off.

I have even been attacked in the street in broad daylight in the middle of Glasgow when out shopping with my family – an incident I will get to a bit later on. I have also had to post plain clothes security guards outside my house after my address appeared on a Celtic fan's internet site. Again, I will explain what happened behind that shameful episode.

The first sign of problems all centred on Donna's flat in Inverkip and around the Gourock area where her family lived.

In the October of my first season at Rangers, her convertible Mini was vandalised outside her parent's house. Someone took a knife to the roof and ripped it to shreds and also smashed the front windscreen. It was terrible for me to see my fiancée's car being wrecked like that, just because her boyfriend played for Rangers.

Donna then decided to take me to the 'Word-Up' club in Greenock one night. That was not the best idea, I have to say, after what went on. I didn't think anything of it beforehand, to be honest. Going into a nightclub with your fiancée and some friends is just a normal thing to do. But it soon became apparent that, as a Rangers player, you couldn't always live a normal life.

When Donna was in the ladies toilet I was waiting outside and this guy just came charging up to me. He was shouting all sorts of things, calling me an 'orange bastard' and a 'f—— arsehole'. I tried to diffuse things. But the guy was just getting worse and worse and people were beginning to stare. A couple of the bouncers came over and there was a bit of an altercation between us. He tried to go for me and I threw a punch to protect myself. It missed him. But the bouncers grabbed him and he was thrown out. Donna and I quickly left. I knew this would not be like Dundee, when you could go out and have a night out without really ever having to worry about getting hassle.

To my astonishment, the papers picked up on the incident a few days later. Some reports claimed there were eyewitnesses saying I was wearing a crucifix outside of my shirt, which I had done to noise people up. Total fabrication. I didn't even own a crucifix. Others said I had a Rangers club tie on and this had wound up some Celtic fans who were in the club. Again this was total rubbish. I knew I would have to start choosing where I socialised far more carefully. It was a real wake-up call.

There were also a couple of problems with my own car having keys taken down it, having the tyres slashed when it was parked outside the flat in Inverkip. I knew we were being targeted, so I started to mix things up a bit and come to Donna's in the club Honda jeep that was given to us by Rangers. Things were calm for a while.

But on Guy Fawkes night we went to Gourock to go to a bonfire and fireworks display with the kids and some of

Donna's family. I took the Honda and parked it at her parents. When we came back from the fireworks display someone had slashed all four tyres on the jeep. I was raging. Clearly it was someone in the area who had watched us park and then done it themselves, or else told someone that was my car. Donna and her family felt bad about it. But it was nothing to do with them.

I have a fairly quick temper, as people will no doubt have worked out from some of my stories in this book, and also some of the red cards I have received in games when I lose the plot and do something rash. I had only been at Rangers for four months and there had now been four or five acts of vandalism. If I could have got my hands on those responsible, I think I would have taken matters into my own hands.

We didn't bother too much with reporting these things to the police. Maybe we should have. But the next incident that happened was far more sinister and we did have to call them in.

In the middle of November I had played and scored my first goal against Celtic in a 2-0 win at Ibrox. I never go out after Old Firm matches into the city and just went back to Donna's flat. We went out for something to eat and came back around 8pm on the Saturday night. Everything was fine. No sign of any problems.

The next day we just lounged around and watched some TV and DVDs. I was very tired after the Celtic game and slept a lot – as I always do after games. On the Sunday night we went out to get a take-away. Both of us jumped into the car and as we drove out the lights shone on the huge fence around the building.

'Novo RIP' had been painted in huge, white letters. Donna

and I still laugh about this now, as my English wasn't the greatest. As I stared at the graffiti I kept saying 'Novo rip, Novo rip'. Donna was like, 'Nacho, that means Rest in Peace. It's what they say when people die!'

I was going off my head. I couldn't believe that someone would do such a thing, daub such a sickening message outside of where your fiancee lived.

We reported it to the police. They came down, took some pictures and a statement on what time we had been going in and out of the flat to try and establish when it happened. Rangers were also very concerned and the club's own security people talked to the police to air their concerns about the amount of things that were going on without anyone ever being caught. That pleased me, but didn't fully put my mind at rest. There was always a lingering fear that things could start up again.

I never got any hassle or had anything vandalised at my own flat in the West End of the city where I stayed at that time and I hoped that the problems in Inverkip and Gourock would die down.

To be fair, things did subside. Then we bought a place in Glasgow for myself, Donna and the boys to live in around four years ago. We moved in as a family for the first time in the summer of 2006. I have said many times that I like Glasgow. The people in the main are decent and honest. But there is always the risk of meeting an idiot head on – and I did big time three years ago.

Myself, Dylan, Ross, Donna and her aunt Maureen had been enjoying a day's shopping in the city centre. We were laden with bags and decided to stop in the Royal Exchange Square Di Maggio's for some lunch. It had been a good family day and we were walking back through Mitchell Lane and onto Mitchell Street, towards where the car was parked. I was out in front, Maureen was behind me and Donna was at the rear trying to hurry the two boys along. Dylan was nine at the time and Ross was six.

Out of nowhere I was aware of this guy running alongside me and the next thing 'bang' he turned, looked at me square on and punched me right on the side of the face.

It's funny looking back on it now. Maureen had ordered a macaroni cheese dish for lunch and it was a massive serving. She had asked the waiter to put it in a box to take home for her husband's dinner that night. In a natural reaction, just as she saw what had happened, Maureen threw the container that had the macaroni cheese at this guy, who was in his thirties, and it smacked him right on the back of the head.

I was dazed. Donna hadn't seen what had happened as it was over so quickly, but Maureen was shouting 'that guy just punched Nacho, he just punched him', as the guy turned and started running back towards the lane. He had been drinking in the pub on the corner. I just flipped. I took off after him and caught up pretty quickly. I flicked out my left foot and tripped him up. I was in a rage. How dare this guy punch me for no reason in front of my family?

I started laying in to him as he scrambled about on the ground. He was outside the door of the pub now and Donna, the kids and Maureen soon arrived and tried to haul me away. Some of the guys who had been in the pub emerged at the door, as did the manager. I stopped hitting the guy and he was held up in the doorway of the pub. I was going mad, shouting and bawling at him. My face was stinging. He had smacked me big time.

The manager of the pub went inside and grabbed the guy's jacket, refusing to let him back in. His pal said to Donna when she asked what the hell he was playing at: 'We were sitting having a pint. He was just looking out the window [when he must have seen us walking by] and he said 'hold on, I'll be back in a minute' before he put his pint down. The next thing he ran out the door and around the corner. He's a Celtic fan. He doesn't like him [pointing to me].'

I found this unbelievable. Basically, the story here was that this guy hated me so much that he would leave his friends whilst having a quiet drink, run outside a bar and sneak up on a footballer and punch him because he didn't like him. I was livid. I had to restrain myself as I wanted to throttle this guy. In front of my family, in front of two young boys who got one hell of a fright and didn't know what was going on.

The manager of the pub said he would call the police and be a witness, give a statement if I wanted to take things further. I looked at the guy in the doorway. How sad. He was wearing what had been a white shirt, but it was all dirty from when he had fallen to the ground, and it had splatters of macaroni on it. I just shook my head and walked away. He muttered: 'I'm sorry, I didn't mean it.' But he had meant it.

As if that whole episode wasn't enough on top of death threats, RIP slogans, car vandalism and all the verbal abuse, there was more to come a couple of years ago in what turned out to be, for me, the most devious and sinister thing yet.

'They've put your address on the internet,' said a close friend in an early evening phone call.

'What?' I asked, unaware of what he was trying to explain to me.

'Nacho, they've put your address on the internet.'

'Who? Where? Why? Bastards! What the...?'

So many thoughts started to go through my mind. What's going to happen now? Will anyone try anything? They better not come near my family. Bastards. A Celtic 'fans' forum had posted my full home address and my car registration number. They were urging people to come and pay me and my family 'a visit'.

The friend who broke the news to me managed to get screen grabs of this hate-filled site, which were then supplied directly to Kenny Scott, Head of Security at Rangers. These were then passed on to the relevant authorities and I was told the site would be shut down and action would be taken.

But I was really concerned about Donna and the boys. I can handle myself and I was not going to be intimidated by anyone, any faceless idiots hiding behind a computer screen. But it's common knowledge when Rangers play all their away games. What if someone came to the house when I was away? I would not have my family under threat.

That night, the club arranged for plain clothes security guys to sit in a car outside my house. I was advised that, for my family's safety, and mine, they would be there around the clock twenty-four hours a day and they would stay in place for two weeks. They parked in different parts of the street, just out of sight, but always keeping an eye on things. It was pretty serious. I couldn't believe it had come to this. But I had no option.

Now I was always under the impression that everything you did online was traceable and accountable. Here we were with conclusive proof of who posted my full home address and my car registration number on a Celtic fans forum. Surely an open and shut case? Well, if anyone was ever arrested over the incident then someone forgot to tell me.

The whole internet saga led to a new song; not quite as sinister as wanting me to die in my sleep from a bullet from the IRA, which was the other one that I used to hear being sung at me during Old Firm games. This new song proclaimed that the Celtic support 'know where you stay Nacho Novo'. And they did. Thanks to some anonymous internet coward. Now every time I make an appearance against Celtic I'm taunted by this song. Sometimes I feel like singing along, as I know where I stay as well!

It can be pretty intense for me at Parkhead; from the minute I step off the team coach until the minute I step back on it. Every time I play there, there is an individual who waits at the side of the bus and abuses me fluently in Spanish when we walk off to go into the stadium – it's as if he goes out of his way to try to offend me. The reality is I am embarrassed for him, he's so driven by hate that he queues up simply to abuse me.

Apparently, according to what he shouts at me, because I am Spanish that must make me a Catholic and as a Catholic I should never have signed for Rangers. I've disgraced my religion by choosing the blue half of Glasgow. The only problem I have with all this is I'm not a Catholic – in fact I'm not very religious at all. That doesn't seem to matter to him though.

On many occasions when visiting Parkhead our players have suffered abuse that's gone way over the top. Fernando Ricksen was once hit by a lighter when trying to take a corner kick. Dr Jackson was hit by a coin when trying to treat an injured Allan McGregor a couple of years ago. I was also hit by a mobile phone, amongst other objects it has to be said, while celebrating an equalising goal that same night. And this is where curiosity gets the better of me.

Why is it OK for someone to wait for our team bus every game and make the vilest of comments without any police action? Why do the same police feel the need to come onto the team bus and speak to me about my allegedly spitting towards Celtic fans, as they did, the same fans that have taunted me? I didn't spit at or towards anyone, as the CCTV evidence proved – I find it sad, though, that those allegations made by such people are treated so seriously, especially when the three individuals who hit Fernando, Dr Jackson and me with missiles are all still at large.

I can understand that it's not always possible to use CCTV images to track down who threw an object, but it can be done, as was proven when Stilian Petrov was hit by a cup at Ibrox during an Old Firm match. The perpetrator found the police waiting for him at the next home game and he was banned for life.

I can accept that it may be difficult to track down who hit Fernando or Dr Jackson but I still can't for the life of me work out why more has not been done in the easier instances to investigate. A mobile phone was thrown at me. Perhaps it was a pay as you go sim card? Perhaps it had absolutely no record of any phone calls ever being made on it? Perhaps it never had any numbers stored such as 'home' for example. But I find that pretty hard to believe. Surely it can't be all that difficult to track down who threw a phone? Maybe I'm underestimating the level of work required for this task.

It must be much more difficult than I imagine although it does make me wonder how any criminals are ever arrested in this country.

Perhaps it's this complete apathy towards finding anyone who wants to target me that breeds confidence in these kinds of people. Certainly, to hear a group of Celtic fans singing about me dying from a bullet from the IRA at an Under 19s Youth Cup Final at Hampden makes me think no one is concerned about the consequences of such behaviour.

Another very low point for me was at Hampden. I attended with my close friend who is a Rangers and Scotland sponsor. He has the best seats in the house at both stadiums and I regularly go and watch Scotland when they play at Hampden. We were making our way inside one evening when some fans sitting to our right spotted us and started singing that old ditty about me being killed by the IRA. What is the relevance of that at a Scotland v Argentina friendly?

Hampden seems to be a place where something always happens. From going to these stadiums you get to know a lot of the stewards and the staff. I had entered the stadium for that Argentina match and spoke to a few of the stewards I know. I put my lounge pass on my blazer lapel and went to my seat. At half time, without thinking, I walked straight to the lounge with my coat zipped up. Countless others had done the same.

One steward took exception to me doing this for obvious reasons and tried to block my path into the lounge but his supervisor escorted me in. Some of my friend's other guests then told me that the steward was fuming that 'just because he's Nacho Novo doesn't mean he doesn't have to show me his badge'.

He knew fine well I had one as he'd seen it earlier that evening. I think I've been at three Scotland games since and the same steward always makes a point of muttering something under his breath. His real issue with me seems to be that I play for Rangers.

That for me is just another example of people in this country getting far too involved in trivial issues when there are far more important things to worry about. I get followed and abused as I head to a lounge by fans who want to sing about me but one steward in particular is more worried about seeing my badge than ensuring good behaviour in the stadium.

It seems to be a recurring theme when I discuss what gets attention in Scotland and what doesn't. The growth of the internet seems to have fuelled a lot of hate. Another phone call from my friend, who had previously brought the publication of my address and car registration to my attention, back in January sounded all too familiar.

He said: 'Have you seen what they've done on the internet this time?'

'Not my address again, pal?'

'No, they've set up a Facebook page looking for a million people to say they hate you.'

I started to laugh; it's all so juvenile and sad.

'That's not all Nacho.'

'What?' I replied wearily knowing that I only got the call because there was more to it.

'They've said some things, some things about you and Javier.'

I lost the plot; Javier, my baby son, was only in this world a matter of days and there was no need to bring him into it.

I tried to calm myself down. However, it was in the wake of the petrol attack on DaMarcus Beasley's car and some internet hard man had decided he wanted my car registration number so he could burn my new baby son and me

190

alive. The words he used to describe my son were vile and I will not repeat them. But the reality of the situation dawned on me. The online Celtic 'fans' community had my car registration number, they had my home address and they had a constant desire to target me.

I will admit that the constant threats do get to you and do make you worry. Here these individuals are, laughing and taking great delight at the notoriety these instances give them. Indeed after issuing my address, the same website changed their homepage to make it look like Google maps with a drop down menu of Rangers people and how to find their address. It obviously didn't give you the information but the lack of concern for what they allowed previously showed through, hence my obvious disappointment that more wasn't done to get the perpetrators.

It perhaps appears that I am bitter about the situation in Scotland and that I feel many things have been done to me with no action taken against the instigators. I will admit there is an element of truth in that.

I sometimes find myself shaking my head in disbelief. Only a few months ago I found myself driving out of the Ibrox car park to be flagged down by a police officer. He pointed out to me that my front windows were tinted and this was not allowed and the next time he was on duty at Ibrox and saw me driving he would have to issue me with a fine and three penalty points unless I had the tints removed. I pointed out to him that I had suffered from victimisation, I had been followed on numerous occasions, my cars had been vandalised and I needed to avoid recognition whilst driving in case it antagonised anyone and led to any type of unsavoury incident.

My protests were to no avail and I was sent on my way well warned about what would happen if I did not remove my tinted windows. One of my teammates has actually just been fined and been issued with points for the same thing. I understand the police have a difficult job to do and I certainly don't want to create any issues for them just because I want my windows tinted. I firmly believe I need the windows tinted in my car to prevent me from being recognised by individuals who may wish to cause me harm. Perhaps, if some of the people who in the past have done me some harm had been brought to justice, then I wouldn't feel like this.

Many people will say that I antagonise the Celtic fans and I bring a lot of these things on myself. It's true that I play with a lot of heart and determination, but I'm not a dirty player, nor am I one to deliberately set out to upset anyone. I quite rightly love Rangers Football Club, I enjoy what I do for a living and I love to win. Therefore I am going to celebrate and enjoy any success we are lucky enough to get. I will not apologise for that.

For me, the biggest issue that causes me to be disliked is the fact I rejected Celtic and always wanted to play for Rangers. It's as if I betrayed the Celtic fans but I did not owe them anything. I wanted to go to Rangers and I'm thankful until this day that I stuck to my guns and got the move that I craved.

I think I can understand why the Celtic fans dislike me so much; after all, I have a decent goal scoring record against them and I rejected them to hold out for a move to Rangers. But my lack of popularity with fans of other clubs has always puzzled me. The Aberdeen fans have never been among my admirers and I was fined £500 and censured very recently by the SFA for reacting with a gesture to the taunts on a visit to Pittodrie.

I find it bizarre the amount of people who take the moral high ground and condemn Rangers fans for singing songs that they find offensive. Football is a sport that's always had an edge to it. Fans of clubs all over the world sing disgusting songs including ones worse than I've ever heard in Scotland. The hypocrisy of the Aberdeen fans would make me laugh if it wasn't so serious.

An element of their fans thinks it's OK to sing about 66 people that died in the Ibrox disaster or about Ian Durrant's injury. It's not, it's vile. Yet they are quick to condemn the Rangers fans. They sing homophobic chants, which are aimed at me, yet act all outraged at my regrettable reaction. I read comments about how it offended young children at the game – were the concerned parents OK with exposing their children to chants of a homophobic nature? The English police investigated Tottenham fans for similar chants aimed at Sol Campbell.

Sadly, in Scotland, it seems only songs that Rangers fans sing are the ones that anyone appears to find very offensive. Our fans are constantly chastised for singing songs or chants but to me it seems like there's a bit of an agenda there, even though there are some songs that our own supporters must stop singing.

Speaking as someone who has been on the receiving end of a lot of these chants, I think that is totally wrong and unacceptable. I have been at Rangers almost six years now and the abuse I've received has been pretty constant in that period. It also always seems to intensify in the aftermath of Old Firm games.

I have developed such a great relationship with the Rangers fans. They loved me for saying no to Celtic – the Celtic fans hated me for it. That was the root of the problem for me.

I've been a target pretty much during my whole career at Rangers and some of the stuff that has happened has really sickened me, although, sadly, it's all part of the downside of being a Rangers player in Glasgow. There are some people in this great city who should be thoroughly ashamed of themselves and their behaviour.

HELICOPTER SUNDAY II

The hangover from the exertions of the previous season lingered on when we returned to Murray Park for the 2008/09 campaign. It was amazing, we only had around a four week break and we were back for training as a result of having a Champions League qualifier to prepare for at the end of July!

That was another consequence of losing the league title. We would have to try and negotiate our way once more through two rounds of the treacherous qualification minefield, but Celtic would gain direct entry into the group stages.

The manager had been a busy man in the early weeks of the summer. He splashed out in excess of £6 million on three strikers: Kenny Miller from Derby County; Kyle Lafferty from Burnley and Andrius Velicka from Viking Stavanger.

I knew Kenny well, of course. He had once been at Rangers, left for Wolves, returned to Celtic and then left for Derby. Now he was coming back to Rangers, the first man to play for one half of the Old Firm twice, and the other once.

I had seen Velicka at Hearts. He was a strong, powerful player who could get a goal. I didn't know much about Lafferty, but again he had a good reputation and many people thought he was a young guy who could have his best years at Rangers.

It was three strikers in the door right away to add to the

competition. We already had Kris Boyd, Daniel Cousin and Jean-Claude Darcheville on board, so either some players would be leaving or there was going to be a fierce battle for starting slots I thought to myself as I looked at the newly assembled striking arsenal at the resumption of pre-season training.

We were drawn against FBK Kaunas in the second round of the Champions League qualifiers. If we dealt with the Lithuanians, then we would have to overcome the Danish champions, Aalborg, to join Celtic with the big boys.

There seemed to be a cloud hanging over us a bit throughout that pre-season. In my opinion it was linked to what had happened at the end of the previous season. We didn't get enough time to clear our heads, to get re-focused and get what had just happened entirely out of our systems.

I also don't think we had enough time to rest our bodies. Some guys had played more than sixty games the season before. It had been gruelling. But here we were just a few short weeks later having to start all over again.

That is not an excuse, as we should have taken care of Kaunas in the opening round. To be knocked out by them was a total embarrassment to everyone at Rangers. There is no way a team from Lithuania should be knocking us out, but that is exactly what happened. After a stuffy 0-0 draw at Ibrox in the first leg, a game in which we were very, very flat, we headed over there for the return.

When Kevin Thomson scored, that should have been it. An away goal and we had enough experience in the team to have seen the job out. But they made it 1-1 with a speculative free kick just before half time. I actually felt we were home and dry in the game. But in the last minute they got a corner out of nothing and scored a header. We had no time to respond. I recall hearing the ref's final whistle and just staring around in utter disbelief.

The season before we had played nineteen games in Europe and reached the UEFA Cup Final. Now, just a couple of months after Manchester, we had been dumped out of Europe for the whole season. No safety net. We were out. It was pretty surreal on the flight on the way home from Lithuania. No one said much. I think we were all in shock.

I knew the fans would be raging at that result. I felt for them. The season before we had taken them on an amazing adventure. But now they had nothing. The only thing we could do to make amends would be to deliver the league title. There were no distractions this time. It would be domestic matters only for us.

I was very close to big Carlos Cuellar, who had been Rangers' Player of the Year and the Scottish Football Writers Player of the Year in 2007/08. I always felt we would struggle to keep a hold of him. When the club moved to sign Madjid Bougherra from Charlton, a centre half, at the start of August, I had a feeling he would be Carlos' replacement.

I was suspended for the first two league games of the season as a result of my disciplinary indiscretions the season before. Carlos was also carrying a hamstring injury and hadn't featured. We were at Falkirk on the opening day of the new season, just days after being sent tumbling out of Europe.

I got wind that Aston Villa was in for Carlos. He had a clause in his contract that allowed him to go if a club offered £8 million. I knew he loved Rangers, but he also harboured ambitions of playing in England, and of getting into the Spanish national team. We spoke at length about his future but I knew in my heart that he would go. It was a fantastic opportunity for him.

Given that our supporters had seen the club sell Alan Hutton to Spurs in the previous January, and then lose the league, and now that Carlos was going off the back of a disastrous European exit, I knew there would be a backlash. People were disillusioned with what was happening. Fans would come up to me in the street and around the city and say 'what's going on in there, wee man'. But we didn't know. It was up to the manager and the club hierarchy to make what moves they felt were right for the team. We had won the opener at Falkirk 1-0 thanks to Velicka's first goal, but that would only be a short-term respite.

Just a few days after Rangers sold Carlos to Villa, the manager made some shrewd moves and splashed the cash. We signed Pedro Mendes from Portsmouth for £3 million and a couple of days later added Steven Davis from Fulham on a permanent deal for around the same money. He also landed Maurice Edu, a young up and coming American internationalist from FC Toronto. The outlay had been in excess of £8.5 million. That was something we had to do. We had brought in quality, and I was delighted to see Steven Davis back as he had been superb on loan for us in the final six months of the previous season.

Daniel Cousin also got his wish of a move to England when he joined Hull City. That move came just the day after we had struck our first serious blow in the title race.

After a decent enough start with wins over Falkirk, Hearts and a draw at Aberdeen, we travelled across the city to take on Celtic in a much earlier than usual first Old Firm clash of the season. Big Daniel put us in the lead with a brilliant individual goal before Samaras equalised. I felt, from my vantage point on the bench, that we had played very well in the game and deserved to be in the lead. The gaffer said at half time to keep that level of performance up and we would get the rewards.

In the second period, we were awesome. Kenny Miller enjoyed the sweet moment of his first goal second time around at Rangers coming against Celtic, and then Pedro scored an absolute screamer to put us 3-1 up. Boruc fumbled to give Kenny his second goal, and we were in dreamland. 4-1 up at Parkhead. We had battered Celtic and let them know that we meant business in this title race, even though they got a late consolation goal to make it 4-2.

On a personal note, I was finding it tough being left on the bench so much. It was hard to pick up the pace of games when you are only getting maybe twenty minutes or half an hour here and there. The tag of 'impact player' was constantly being used – much to my frustration, as that was not how I wanted to be viewed.

It was tough with so many players competing for slots. Between the Celtic game at Parkhead at the end of August and the turn of the year we played eighteen games – and I only started six times, appearing on ten occasions from the bench and not being involved at all in the other two games. That was a real source of frustration for me. I wanted to play!

The fact I only scored four times in that period as well, for me, was a reflection of the fact I need to be getting a regular starting run for a goals return. I did speak with the manager, he knew my frustrations, but there were other players in the squad in the same position. With no Europe, the injuries were not as bad and people had time to prepare and rest more in the midweeks that had been freed up. That said, even though I was not happy on a personal level at not getting more starts, the team was doing very well.

We went on a solid SPL run, just the kind of consistent form that you need if you want to be champions. We were racking up three points most weeks, bar a shock 1-0 defeat at St Mirren, and we also made it through to the semi-finals of the League Cup with wins over Partick Thistle and Hamilton Accies.

Celtic, however, were using all their experience. They were grinding out wins, applying as much pressure as possible on us. We knew we would have to stay in touch with the next Old Firm game at our place just two days after Christmas. A damaging 2-1 defeat at Hearts and then a 2-2 draw away at Dundee United were two dreadful results just when we didn't need them. When Celtic came to Ibrox, they were four points clear. It was a huge match for both teams.

As can often happen when Rangers vs Celtic matches are built up in the press and media, this one was not the greatest. Neither side really created much in the way of chances, although Kris Boyd went through one on one with Boruc and lost out in that duel when he made the save.

That came not long into the second half. And Celtic went straight up the park and hit us with a killer blow. A hopeful ball from the back was nodded on by Samaras, and Scott McDonald managed to turn Kirk Broadfoot. McDonald was always a dangerous player, he was a real goalscorer. And he lashed a volley past Allan McGregor to put them into the lead.

I always felt it would be one of those Old Firm matches decided by just one goal. It was. Celtic headed back across the city with a seven-point lead and many said that the league title was over. I must admit it was hard to get our heads up after that. We had been motoring along in a decent position, then bang. A couple of bad results and Celtic were stretching clear.

The one thing about Walter Smith was that he never panicked. He was keen on team meetings, and still is, when things are not going well and it can be beneficial for everyone to air their views. We spoke about the situation we were in. He told us nothing was over. There was a lot of football to come, including two Old Firm games. But we had to play every match like a cup final.

Early in the New Year, Birmingham City – managed by my old gaffer Alex McLeish – made a £3.5 million bid for Kris Boyd. It was a bolt from the blue, but more was to follow. The chairman and the manager spoke quite openly in the press that a player would have to be sold in the January window as the club needed to bring in money. This shocked the players. You tend not to take much to do with club affairs and business, focusing on the one thing you can control, which is the game. But the players did get a bit uneasy as, quite clearly as it had been stated, someone would have to go. It was the first signal that all wasn't well behind the scenes and, naturally, this did concern me.

Firstly, we were locked in a title race with Celtic. OK, we were seven points adrift, but what impact would it have if we had to sell a top player? And what message would it send to the fans? Only a year ago they had watched Alan Hutton go when we were battling with Celtic and no one came in. It was a very long month. The speculation in the press was rife, with just about everyone being linked with a move away.

The manager told us to blank it out and get on with playing football. Those situations are when you see Walter Smith at his best. He protected the players, kept a steady ship, even though he knew himself that things were not going well financially. It would have been easy for a manager to say 'hey, I'm not putting up with this' and walk out. But he knew how much Rangers needed him.

Ironically, against the backdrop of all this uncertainty, we hit top form. We beat Inverness 3-0 away from home and then racked up victories in the league against Falkirk and Dundee United. We also made it through to the League Cup Final – where we would face Celtic in March – after beating Falkirk 3-0 at Hampden. I scored two goals that night, continuing my good luck in that competition and at the national stadium after I was given a rare starting slot by the manager.

Like every Rangers fan, I counted down the hours to the closure of the transfer window. Despite the warnings that we would have to sell, despite the huge interest in many of our players, no one went. Boydy knocked back Birmingham, which I was delighted about. It had concerned me how we were possibly going to replace the best goal-scorer in the league. There was a huge weight off the players' shoulders. Although results had suggested otherwise, we were worried. We knew we had a real chance of clawing back Celtic. But had one or two players gone, it would have upset everyone and left us weakened. But nobody was sold. We regrouped and got on with the battle.

Celtic and ourselves were neck and neck, going at it hammer and tongs. When we met in the League Cup Final on 15 March, everyone claimed it would be a pointer as to where the league title would end up. It was also the first trophy of the season, which was very important. Celtic had gone out of the Scottish Cup and couldn't win the treble, but we could, if we won the League Cup.

The game itself was probably one of our biggest regrets of that season, that and the European disaster in Kaunas. We just never got going that afternoon. Celtic were the better side and looked the more likely to score. It was one of those performances that can just crop up from time to time that are inexplicable. We had been in good form, we were confident. But we just never turned up. They weren't much better, and the game, if truth were told, was hardly a decent advert for the best two teams in the country.

When Celtic scored the first goal through an O'Dea header in the first period of extra time, we didn't even muster much of a fight-back. That was just inexcusable in any cup final, but especially one against your fiercest rivals. McGeady scored a penalty late on to seal the game and we trudged away with our heads down. A 2-2 draw with Hearts at home in the league just six days later suggested we would have to get the Old Firm defeat out of our system quickly. But there was another storm heading our way . . .

The international break for two weeks after that Hearts draw was supposed to be the period when those of us not away playing for our countries would re-group. Unfortunately, by the time we got the whole squad back together a fortnight later, chaos had ensued.

Barry Ferguson and Allan McGregor had been away with Scotland and had stayed up all night having a drink after the defeat to Holland in Amsterdam. There were other players involved, but they carried the can for most of it and it was splashed all over the press. Most managers would probably have sent them home, but George Burley opted to keep them in the squad for the game against Iceland the following midweek. Barry and Allan, of course, then made their now infamous gestures and were getting it in the neck from everywhere.

To be honest, and I think this would normally apply at all clubs, players stick together. Barry and Allan were not only two top class performers for us, Barry being skipper, but they were also very popular boys in the dressing room. We knew they were taking all the flak when others had been involved. They had made mistakes, of course they had, but it was open season on them. When they came in to Murray Park that Friday morning, we would have had a bit of banter, but they would have been made to feel back amongst their own. However, neither of them saw much of the dressing room.

They were called out by the manager and sent home. As the day developed, they were told they would not play again for the team. I remember being at home and watching the whole episode unfold on TV. My first instinct was to feel gutted for the boys. They were my teammates and I had a lot of time for them both. Clearly something had gone on that the manager was not pleased about and it was his right to do whatever he felt necessary. I just worried about the impact it would have.

We were into the last eight weeks of the season and, having survived the transfer window uncertainty, this would be yet more turmoil. We were losing two experienced players and that would be hard on the squad. But the manager did what he did for his reasons. I never spoke to Barry or Allan about what had happened. They were both sent away for a couple of weeks. The message from the management was clear. No matter the distractions, we had a league to try and win.

We faced Falkirk on the Sunday and managed to scrape a 1-0 win. After everything that had just happened with the whole 'Boozegate' affair, it was probably our most important win of that season. I think all eyes were on us that day, waiting to see if we would fail, if the impact of losing Barry and Allan would de-rail us. We had to show a lot of bottle. I was proud of the team that day, and the fans. They got right behind us when we needed them most. Maybe a siege mentality set in, I don't know. But from that day on we just threw our shoulders back. It was as if nothing, no chain of events or troubles internally, were going to stop us from chasing the dream of the championship. We wanted it that badly.

In the next four games, we took a maximum return of twelve points. We beat St Mirren, Motherwell, Hibs and Hearts. We also beat St Mirren in the semi-final of the Scottish Cup to book another date at Hampden. By the time we faced Celtic on 9 May at Ibrox, we were a point behind with four games to play. It was a must win for us. My mind drifted back to 2005 when we had lost a game to them when the circumstances were the same. However, this time there was to be no repeat.

Steven Davis scored just before half time with an excellent goal after a great move. We had a lead and we did not let it go. I felt we wanted it more than Celtic that day and we got the rewards. We jumped above them into first position. Two points clear with three games left. In the box seat. Having been through two nail-biting climaxes to a season before, I should have been prepared. But the nerves were unbelievable.

When you get to that stage of a season, when you know how close you are – and how fatal one slip can be – then it's very difficult not to be affected. Training can be edgy, the management have to try and keep things nice and low key, even though they are feeling it inside as well. We faced Hibs at Easter Road in the midweek after beating Celtic. The night before, Celtic had defeated Dundee United at Parkhead to go a point ahead of us again. We had watched some of the game in our hotel. We had no margin for error. Hibs away is always a tough fixture, and they were right up for the game from the off. Derek Riordan scored an excellent goal to put them 1-0 up and we were staring down the barrel of a quite disastrous result. The gaffer threw me on from the bench and we started to have a real go, pinning Hibs back. We swept forward, attack after attack. There was no grey area. We needed a goal.

Midway through the second period, after another onslaught, we had a corner. The ball came in and was pinging around the box. One of our boys got a shot away and the Hibs keeper, Makalamby, made a great save. I got a connection on the rebound and tried to force it over the line. They had a player standing on the line and he booted it clear – but from where I was it had already crossed the line. I was certain it was a goal. I looked across at the assistant ref and he started running back as if it was a goal. Then he stopped. Then he ran back a bit. It was chaos. I went off my head and ran over to give him both barrels. I was convinced that the ball was over the line. In fact, until the day I die no one will ever tell me differently. The ball was in. But he didn't give it.

I couldn't believe we were not awarded a goal and that only added to the drama of what was happening for us. We kept battering away at Hibs' goalmouth, and they kept trying to hit us on the counter. Then, I did get my goal. Another scramble in the box. This time I got there first and slammed it home.

I wheeled away. It had come at the end where I scored the goal that clinched us the title back in 2005. This one hadn't done that, but it might have saved us. I always fancy Rangers to go on and get a second in those situations, when we get the impetus of a goal and with the fans behind us we normally kick on. But we could not get the breakthrough. The game ended 1-1. We were locked on eighty points with Celtic – but they had the better goal difference of plus two. It was in their hands. The whole way back from Edinburgh I was still raging about the goal that never was. I was on the phone to friends asking what the TV had shown. I was convinced we had suffered from a bad call, one that could have cost us the title.

We had little time to dwell on matters, as Aberdeen were next up on the Saturday. We had to win. And we had to score goals. Again, the match was laced with controversy.

Kyle Lafferty went down after a challenge with the Aberdeen player Charlie Mulgrew and he was sent off when there was nothing in it. Kyle let himself down that day and came out and admitted as much later when he apologised. We had Madjid Bougherra sent off and it looked as though it would be the day things slipped away.

In the second half, though, we started to get going. Kenny Miller scored twice in quick succession, but we switched off and allowed Aberdeen to score. It was a funny feeling that day. We had won the game and gone three points clear of Celtic, who were due to face Hibs the next day. But we had only cut their goal difference by one. They had destiny in their own hands, and we had to wait and wonder. Hibs had damaged us. Now we had to hope they could do the same to Celtic. And, in yet another twist in the crazy game that football can be, they did exactly that.

On the Sunday, at Easter Road, Celtic were held to a 0-0 draw. They had dropped two crucial points and we had it in our own hands again. Two points clear going into the final day. Rangers away at Dundee United; Celtic at home to Hearts. They had the better looking of the fixtures in terms of judging the size of the task. We had a very poor record at Tannadice. But, unlike the last two occasions I had been involved in when it had gone right down to the final day, we had the destination of the SPL title under out own control. Win and we were champions. I said it over and over in my head all week as Helicopter Sunday II edged ever closer.

Now it can be a dangerous thing to go into press conferences and say silly things. The press have a job to do. They look for the headline. I have never had a problem speaking honestly to journalists – it's part of your job. But, especially in that situation, you have to be careful. The manager stressed to us that we had to keep the head down and say nothing silly in the papers. We knew what was on the line and the last thing we needed was to give Celtic any more motivation. Obviously, someone forgot to tell Georgios Samaras that.

We all saw the headlines in the papers. He basically said that, even if we went on to hold firm on the Sunday at Tannadice and win the league, Celtic had been the better team all season. They played better football, and deserved to be champions. I could not believe that a fairly experienced guy would have made such statements. Not that we needed any extra edge, but the cuttings were duly pinned up on the dressing room wall.

The night before the game we settled into our hotel. It was a pretty nervous evening, with everyone just anxious for the next day to come. As part of our preparations, we were shown a video by the management; I think it was Ally McCoist who was behind it, of the Celtic players celebrating in the dressing room the season before at Tannadice after they had won the title on the last day. McGeady and one or two others were having a joke at our expense. We were determined not to let that happen again.

I could not recall seeing a team as fired up as we were that day. We had to go for United from the off, ensure that events at Parkhead did not matter. If we beat United, the title was ours. Inside the first few minutes, Kyle Lafferty swept us into the lead. I was on the bench and we just exploded with joy. We absolutely destroyed United. The pace of our game, the aggression, you could just tell we knew what was on the line. Pedro Mendes then scored a superb second goal and we went in 2-0 up. It was still 0-0 between Celtic and Hearts.

The manager was delighted with the first forty-five minutes, but stressed to us that we could not come down through the gears. There was no chance of that. Into the second half and a brilliant move ended with Boydy slamming the ball home to make it 3-0. The minute that goal went in, I knew we were champions. Our fans were going crazy. What an atmosphere.

We saw the game out quite easily and when the final whistle blew it was just an explosion of joy! People have asked me since what was the better of the two last day triumphs, 2005 or 2009? I loved them both! But they were very different.

In 2005, the whole thing turned inside a minute when Celtic lost two goals at Motherwell. For sheer drama, that will never be topped. Four years later, it was a different kind of drama.

But it was sweet, so sweet. As we went around with the trophy that had arrived in plenty of time by helicopter, the fans were singing 'Ha Ha Samaras' in reference to his comments. I decided to join in, and shouted it live in a few radio interviews that the other boys were doing on the lap of honour. Why not? If you want to give out stick, then you have to take it back. I have learned that the hard way as well at times. He was disrespectful in what he said about Rangers and had to eat his words.

We headed back to Ibrox for a party. Again, it was amazing. Tens of thousands of fans in the stadium to welcome us. It was quite emotional, really. All the effort of a long season and you see the joy on the faces of everyone from the manager down through all the staff, the kit-man Jimmy Bell, all the staff at Ibrox. And, of course, the fans. I was so thrilled we had done it for them, especially after what had happened a year before.

We still had the Scottish Cup Final against Falkirk to come, which would be the chance to land the double. It was hard to get back down to earth again after the high of the weekend before, but again the management team stressed to us that this would be the final game of the season, it was a Cup Final and there was no way we wanted to lose and go out on a damp squib. The game, as I had expected, wasn't up to much. We were flat. I think the exertion of the week before had certainly taken its toll.

I was put on at half time in place of Boydy. From the kick off, the ball dropped over on my side and went out for a throw in. It was taken quickly and as I turned the ball just sat up beautifully. I thought to myself 'I am hitting this'. From the moment it left my boot, I knew it was in. From around forty yards, the ball travelled, swerved and dipped over the Falkirk keeper and into the net. We were 1-0 up. It was all we needed.

When the final whistle blew it was relief, joy, tiredness – all sorts of feelings rolled into one. We had the domestic double. That was our reward for a season in which we had given absolutely everything. There had been many highs and lows; it had been yet another roller coaster. But it had been the best. We were champions. And we deserved it. No matter what anyone else tried to say.

15

OH DONNA

Footballers' private lives have not been far from the head-lines over the past few years. It now seems there is as much interest in what we do and how we live as pop stars and actors!

I have always tried to keep my own business to myself and, in the main, that has been the case, thankfully. I think it's important to be able to get on with things with your family away from the media glare, the focus that is very much on you as a Rangers player.

I have a very content home life with my fiancée, Donna, the two boys Dylan and Ross, and my pride and joy, my son Javier, who arrived in January. We are a close unit and we all get on extremely well.

Unfortunately, there have been some misleading stories about how Donna and myself got together, and I want to set the record straight on exactly what happened. As much as it's our business, I want people to know the truth, as what appeared in the press about us was inaccurate and disappointing.

I first met Donna when I moved to Raith Rovers from Spain. As I have explained at the start of my story, I arrived in Scotland in 2001 and hardly knew anyone. I think a lot of people maybe felt sorry for me as I couldn't speak a word of English and looked out for me. Two of those people were Ross Mathieson, my teammate at Raith, and his girlfriend at the time, Donna.

I would go around to their place, have some dinner with them or a take-out pizza, and Donna would help me learn English. There was no romance or anything between us, not a hint. She was Ross's girlfriend, they had two kids, and I looked on both of them as friends. Good friends at that.

We all hung out together for the year I was at Raith and I enjoyed the social circle that was there along with the other boys at the club at the time and their wives and partners. As I have said, these people were more or less all I had as it was always going to be difficult to meet friends outwith my immediate football circle as I didn't know anyone in Kirkcaldy!

When I moved to Dundee I still stayed in touch with Ross and Donna. I would come down from Dundee for the odd night and stay over if we went out for a few drinks or whatever. I am being absolutely truthful here – I looked on Donna as a friend as much as I did Ross.

As time moved along, I was aware that they were having some problems in their relationship. I was not involved in that and I did not want to be involved. What happens between two people is their business. I was worried for them both as I didn't want to see my friends go through a break-up, especially with the kids involved. Having gone through the situation myself with my own parents, I would not wish that scenario on anyone.

I could go into a lot of the stuff that went on between them, events that I have been made aware of since they happened, but I don't want to publicly talk about something that was, when all is said and done, the business of Donna and Ross.

What I do want to do is clarify how we started our relationship. The press stories claimed that I had gone behind Ross's back and had an affair with Donna when they were still a couple. The image that was painted in these stories was that I had stolen my former teammate's girlfriend away and that I was the bad guy in all of this. Nothing could be further from the truth of what actually happened.

Donna had moved away from the home they had in Kirkcaldy and into her flat in Inverkip to be close to her family in Gourock. They had officially separated for at least six months before we started our relationship, just around the time that I signed for Rangers in the summer of 2004. So there was no sneaky affair. There was no attempt from me to break them up. Donna and I were friends and it grew into something else. This happened long after they had split up. That is the truth of the matter.

We took things very slowly when we started our relationship. Although I had known Donna for a few years, we had never looked on each other in a romantic way. But as time went on we started to grow closer and closer and it just blossomed from there. She stayed down in Inverkip with the boys and I had my house in Glasgow. We had that set-up for two years and it was 2006 before we got a house that we all moved into as a family.

It was a big responsibility for me to come into the lives of Dylan and Ross. That is not a situation you can just take lightly. If you are going to be around kids every day as they grow up, then you have to be the right kind of influence on them and try to help them grow up in the right way. I have always tried to do my best by them in the six years that I have been their mother's partner. I treat the boys in the same way as I will treat Javier. They are two cracking kids. They both play football for local teams, they have good personalities and I just try to be there for them whenever they need me.

As for Donna, we have always got on very well. We have an excellent relationship and when Javier arrived earlier this year it only served to bring us even closer together. I was so proud of her the day he was born and she has given me a beautiful son.

Family has always been important to me. I think people will have gleaned that from what I have said in this book about my upbringing and my relationship with my own mother and my sister. I want all of us – Donna, Dylan, Ross and Javier – to have that kind of family unit and all be there for each other at all times.

We try to live as normal a life as possible. It's not all glamour as people think it is when they watch shows like *Footballer's Wives*! Donna is just a down to earth Scottish girl! I know not to mess with her, but she also knows that we Spaniards can be fiery! We have a mutual love and respect for each other and that is the foundation of our relationship, and we plan to get married.

We do normal things, go for dinner, and go to the movies. I like to get the boys the latest games for their Playstations or X-boxes. We have the busy schedule of taking the boys to and from school, to and from football training and games – all pretty routine family stuff.

Donna and the boys know that I like to sleep a lot when I come in from training and games – although that has not been all that possible since Javier's arrival! I have to admit that nothing prepared me for that. The sleepless nights certainly didn't have me as sharp as I could have been in the morning before matches, but I got through it! And Donna is always quick to remind me that it's part of my job now as a dad. You have to put the shift in!

Just a few days after Javier was born I scored a late goal to win the game 1-0 against Hamilton Accies. It was in my head beforehand that I would do the cradling-the-baby celebration that was made so famous by the Brazilian striker Bebeto many years ago at the World Cup. I got the chance to do that, and afterwards in the press conference I dedicated the goal to Javier, which made me very proud.

Of course, one of the biggest regrets for me is that my mum is not around to see Javier. She would have just adored him. It makes me very sad sometimes when I think about how he won't have a grandma on my side. These are the painful issues you have to go through when you lose a parent at such a young age. But I will ensure that Javier knows all about his grandma and what kind of person she was as he gets older. He has an Aunt Arantxa, and my sister came over just after he was born to be with us. It was a very emotional time for us, after everything that we have been through in our lives and, of course, losing mum.

I have been asked a few times already if I want Javier to be a footballer! He could even play for Scotland as he was born here, some of the fans have said to me! I only wish for him to be happy, healthy and enjoy his life. Donna and myself will support him, and Dylan and Ross, on whatever path they choose to go down.

The fact I have had my own son did also bring the issue of my own relationship with my dad back into focus. We had a complete breakdown in relationship in the aftermath of his split-up from my mother, as I have explained. There was a lot of anger on my part. But at the end of last year we had some conversations on the phone. Bit by bit we might be able to find some common ground again. We'll see what happens. At the end of the day, he is my dad. I have that bond now with Javier and I know what it means. Families have issues, I am not the only one to have gone through troubled times.

But I feel I am a better man now for everything that I have had to deal with. With my Donna and the three boys around me, I feel happy, content and look forward to wherever the rest of my life goes.

MY GREATEST GERS XI

I have been honoured to have played alongside many fantastic players in my six years at Rangers; I have also worked under three managers.

Being a good teammate, being committed to those who pull on the jersey in the dressing room and go into battle has always been central to my make-up – and it has also been a trait of many of the guys I have worked with.

It was never going to be an easy task to try and pick a best ever team as, in truth, I could probably have picked two line-ups from the kind of top class and quality players that I have had as teammates.

But I haven't shirked the tackle. I have opted for a 4-3-3 formation, and also chosen a man to be the leader. To anyone who thinks they should have been in the team, I apologise!

ALLAN McGREGOR
This was a very difficult decision. Rangers have been blessed over the years with a plethora of excellent goalkeepers. During my time alone we've had Klos, Allan and Neil Alexander. Allan has been the number one during the majority of that time and has put in many match-winning performances (as did Neil, especially on run to UEFA Cup Final).

He has improved greatly and his short stopping at times has been extremely valuable in terms of points. Any successful team needs to have a goalkeeper whom they have confidence in and Allan certainly inspires that. He's been at Rangers for a long period now and has rightly made the position his own.

He's a good lad and a great goalkeeper and hopefully he'll be fulfilling the role for many years to come. He's kept us in games we didn't deserve to take anything from and some of his saves have helped inspire the team to push that little bit extra. As with the rest of the squad, he has a desire to win and he's an important member of the camp.

STEVIE SMITH

Again, this was a very closely fought battle between Stevie and Sasa Papac. Sasa for me has been one of our most consistent players over recent years and has transformed himself into an excellent full back. His coolness in possession and in pressure situations meant that there was very little to choose between him and Stevie. His composure in that penalty shoot out in Florence will live with me forever.

Stevie is a product of the youth development that has become more and more important to Rangers in recent years. He progressed through the ranks at the same time as Alan Hutton and it's testament to the work of the coaches at the club that two full backs as good as Stevie and Alan have come through the ranks.

Where Stevie has struggled in recent years has been due to injury and it's very difficult to get match fit and get the run of games you need in those circumstances. The exceptional level of consistency shown by Sasa has hampered any opportunities he has had at getting back into the team.

As a person Stevie is a moaner but he's a good guy with a Rangers background and he knows how much this club means to the fans. At times the young players coming through have an extra burden of expectation on their shoulders from the fans and it takes a strong individual to cope with that. To thrive at a big club, and we are one of the biggest, takes mental toughness and Stevie has that.

I fully expect Stevie to go on to have a very successful career as an attacking full back – he has all the attributes required to keep on playing at such a massive club.

CARLOS CUELLAR

What can you say about Carlos? Simply an unbelievable defender. With our backs to the wall in Bremen and Florence, just to name two occasions, he was colossal. Without Carlos we simply wouldn't have been competing in a UEFA Cup Final that year.

I have to say that again, like with the goalkeeping position, Rangers have been blessed with some exceptional talent and some amazing characters during my time at centre half. Madjid Bougherra is a great defender and is performing at the same consistent level that Carlos achieved. It is astonishing given the current climate surrounding the club which has been fairly prevalent over the last six years that I can leave someone as good as Madjid out of my team. Perhaps I should have tried to accommodate him at right wing such is the excellent attacking dimension he brings to the team!

For me though, Carlos just edges it for my eleven. That night in Bremen I started up front on my own in a 4-5-1 system and to be honest I didn't see much of the ball! The never say die attitude the team displayed that night filled me with confidence and suggested to me we had the character to go all the way to the final.

Bremen threw everything they had at us that night with Klasnic and Diego, amongst others, being particularly dangerous. That performance must collectively rank as one of our best defensive performances ever and Carlos was simply immense.

He just got better and better in every game he played and again in Florence he marshalled Mutu, Liverani and eventually Vieri. Alongside Davie Weir he excelled and I was gutted to see him leave. His transfer to Aston Villa happened so quickly. Just days before I had travelled through to see our game away to Falkirk. Carlos had been at Murray Park for treatment and then met us through there. The reception we got from the fans that day was, as always, exceptional and I think it still disappoints Carlos that that was his final goodbye.

I still hear from Carlos fairly regularly, especially before big games and, like me, Rangers are definitely in his heart.

DAVID WEIR
Inspirational.

Davie Weir must be the best role model in Scottish football for any aspiring young player. He is the model professional and it's testament to his professionalism and the quality of life and preparation he has that he still plays at the top level at his age.

People were amazed that Davie played almost every game in the season we got to the UEFA Cup Final. I don't think we could have played more game time that season if we tried. Replays in Scottish Cup, extra time and penalties in every cup. It was remarkable how many games we had to play that season. It was also disappointing how many games we had to play in such a tight period of time, which ultimately robbed us of more success. However, Davie featured in so many of those games and here we are three years later and he's still performing week in, week out for the club.

Many observers perhaps thought Davie, like Ugo (another good player and guy) would only be at the club a matter of months – to steady the ship when the Gaffer came back. That Davie has exceeded those expectations and proved so many people wrong is something he should be proud of.

My biggest regret is that Davie Weir didn't arrive at Rangers much earlier.

For the last central defensive spot Davie was run close by another remarkable man, Marvin Andrews. 'Helicopter Sunday' will never be forgotten by the fans or by any of us who were involved that day. As everyone knows, Marvin is a man of great faith and he told everyone to keep believing – well we did and it was such a touching moment to hear the uproar amongst the fans when Motherwell had scored to look at Marvin and see him thanking God.

ALAN HUTTON

Another player that sadly is no longer at the club. Alan had a tough time with injuries and form at Rangers but ultimately showed just how good a player he is. This culminated in a transfer to the Premiership in a big money move.

As I discussed earlier in relation to Stevie Smith, it is very difficult for the young Scottish lads who have been brought through with huge expectation and have so many friends who support the club – it's hard for them to escape the pressure. Alan went through turbulent times and was well down the pecking order when Walter returned to the club.

Walter managed to restore Alan's confidence and had him playing with a swagger. Much like Madjid does now, Alan drove down the wing to great effect and many good teams struggled to defend against him. His ability has led to him being one of Scotland's most important players now as well.

Like in other positions there has been much competition for the right back slot. Both Steven Whittaker and Kirk Broadfoot have done fantastically well when played there. Steven has suffered a little in that he's so versatile and has played in so many positions. Kirk has adapted well to playing at full back and always puts in consistent performances. However, Alan just edges it for me given his ability to combine the attacking side of the game to being such a good defender as well, often being found coming round the back of the centre halves to avert any danger.

Whilst Alan has struggled since moving to Spurs due to the depth of their squad I'm sure he'll keep progressing – he's simply too good a player not to be playing at the top level. He's been a big miss and I hope he starts to show the form that won him a big money transfer to the Premiership.

ALEX RAE
Born and bred a bluenose.

Alex signed for Rangers about the same time as me. We both made our debuts on a pre-season trip to the Austrian mountains and he knew exactly what it meant to play for Rangers. It was another exciting time at the club as we also signed Jean Alain Boumsong on a Bosman – another fantastic defender! I scored two goals against Roma in Kapfenberg and Alex scored a second half penalty. As always the fans had followed us to the Austrian mountains and it was great to score in front of them against such good opposition.

Football at times can be a battle and it was good to know you had a warrior like Alex on your side rather than up against you. Playing for Rangers means everything to me; I can only imagine how good it must have felt for Alex after living all of his life as a Rangers man. The emotion on his face when the crowd went crazy indicating that Motherwell had scored on 'Helicopter Sunday' summed up what it meant to him.

What people forget about guys like Alex because of their style of play is that he's actually an excellent footballer. He had a good touch, could pass a ball and most importantly he won the ball – an attribute that's vital in any team. You want a midfield that dominates and doesn't get bullied; Alex would ensure that wouldn't happen.

Alex and I both arrived at the club at the same time and both enjoyed that first league success at the same time. A bit like Davie Weir in that I wish Rangers got the benefit of Alex's talents over a longer period of time. And I'm sure Alex would have thrived and thoroughly enjoyed a longer period at the club he loves.

BARRY FERGUSON

Barry is a bigger moaner than Stevie Smith. Seriously, he doesn't stop whining. Even when he was playing. But he can play. Never scared of the ball, never hid away. It's a bit of a recurring theme but young Scottish players who are nurtured by this club have a higher level of expectation on them than other players. I can't put my finger on why that's the case but it just seems to be the way it is.

Barry can control a game and keeps the ball moving. He leads by example and his form suffered for a period, especially on road to the UEFA Cup Final, because he was playing through a horrendous injury. It's testament to his determination and attitude that he kept playing. Many other players would have taken the easy route of going for an operation or having a period of rest. I'm like Barry in many ways in that I don't want to be injured and will play through the pain barrier – even when we shouldn't!

Barry is showing now at Birmingham just how good a player he is – too many people in Scotland took his ability for granted. Barry has always taken a lot of abuse and many Scotland fans blamed him for years for Scotland's ills. Alongside Darren Fletcher, who is now emerging as a phenomenal player, Barry is Scotland's best midfielder and he should be involved at that level. It's a strange situation in Scotland where people seem to take great pleasure in their 'own' failing or not doing well. Barry has suffered more than most from people who want to knock him for the sake of it.

If it were up to me he'd be one of the first names on my team sheet whoever I was manager of.

STEVEN DAVIS

I haven't just selected Davo because he is one of my closest friends – I have picked him as he is quite simply an outstanding footballer. He arrived at the club on loan from Fulham in 2008 and right away you could see the class he had. He is such an intelligent player, has great skill and can pick a pass out of nothing. He scored some crucial goals over that loan period, and I really hoped it would be possible for the club to sign him on a permanent basis after that. I knew he had grown up as a Rangers fan and loved the club. He had supported the team all his life and was living the dream pulling on a blue jersey. It took a bit of time to get him back for good, but I was thrilled when he returned in the summer of 2008. He is a Premiership class midfielder and we are really lucky to have him. I have lost count of the number of times I have made runs and he finds you with the perfect pass. He is a forward player's dream with the weight of pass he supplies and his vision. My big fear is that some English teams will come back and try to tempt him to move down south again. He would be a huge loss to Rangers as he brings so much on and off the pitch. Steven is also a tremendous guy. He has been a good friend for me and his friendship has always meant a lot.

SHOTA ARVELADZE
What a dancer . . .

Shota Arveladze was a superb player for Rangers. He was so skilful and effective and played in so many different positions during his time with the club.

He could change a game in an instant and it was a pleasure to play alongside him. It was guys like him and Zurab Khizanishvili who really helped me settle in at Rangers and it was an honour to play alongside him.

Shota would provide the creative edge I feel you need in

226

any team and would float behind the strikers and in front of midfield. He could score some outrageous goals and I think he was much underrated as a player. I think he complemented both Dado Prso and me very well and that was my best season at the club in terms of a goals return as I was starting games consistently and in my favoured position. Shota was a very unselfish player and created so many chances for other players.

He was another player that I wish was at Rangers for longer as he had so much to offer. This club is magical in that it becomes so important to so many foreign players who come here. Shota was another, like myself, who found himself with such a strong bond to this wonderful club and he'll always love the club.

His dancing at Easter Road on Helicopter Sunday will live with me forever – just another funny anecdote from one of the best days of my life.

DADO PRSO

I used the word when describing Alex Rae, but it is also apt for Dado, and that word is warrior. Dado signed for the club at the same time as me, Alex and Boumsong and he was an excellent signing. Again, I'm sure every Rangers fan wishes he'd signed for the club much earlier.

Dado Prso is the best forward I have every played with – he created so much for me and won us games on his own. He put his body through so much punishment and as a result his career ended much sooner than he deserved.

My team is packed full of players who you'd want on your side in a football battle and Dado typifies that. Who can forget the Old Firm game where Dado took a bad head knock only to return and dominate the game with a bandaged head? That kind of thing is inspirational for the players and it drives you on to play for your teammates.

The team spirit we had with Dado is much like it is just now – very strong. Dado though was an exceptional person and another who felt truly honoured every time he wore the blue jersey – I think that showed in the way he played. A firm favourite with the fans and teammates alike, he brought an attitude, ability and determination that drove us through games and got us points where we may otherwise have missed out.

The only bad thing I'd say about Dado is that his singing is up there with Shota's dancing. Dado singing and Shota dancing on the bus on the way back to Ibrox with the SPL trophy in 2005 still makes me laugh to this day.

NACHO NOVO

There's not much I'm going to say as to why I picked myself – simply because I can and it's my team!

I love playing for Rangers and love playing for the fans. Playing with those players and for that manager would and always has been an honour for me.

There were so many good players that I've had to leave out especially up front. What can you say about Kris Boyd? He just simply scores goals for fun. His record is simply phenomenal. His exclusion is no slight on him, rather a major tribute to Dado Prso and Shota Arveladze who just pipped him to the forward positions alongside yours truly! Also, Peter Lovenkrands deserves a special mention purely for his amazing knack of scoring in big games.

MANAGER: WALTER SMITH

Legend.

Walter Smith is Rangers. What he has done for this club in his two spells in charge cannot be underestimated.

As a player you do not always agree with the manager's decisions – usually when you don't play! However, he is a great man and one who you would run your heart out for. His footballing record speaks for itself but off the park he is a great man and one I have so much respect for.

With all the uncertainty over the club from a financial aspect in the past year it is reassuring to have someone like him in control. No other manager could have steered this club through such a difficult period. He is calm and authoritative and has done a remarkable job in very trying circumstances.

With the starting eleven above and the strength on the bench and in the dugout with the greatest manager I've ever played under, my team would be very successful. It would have been nice to see that eleven play together in their prime.

17

TRUE BLUE

'Once a Ranger, always a Ranger' . . .

'Don't be a stranger, be a Glasgow Ranger' . . .

'Rangers fans are born, not manufactured. Those who understand need no explanation, those who don't, don't matter' . . .

These are only a few of the famous sayings linked to this magnificent club. I agree with them, although technically I wasn't born a Rangers fan; nor was I manufactured a Rangers fan. But I dare anyone to spend any time in this institution and not then have Rangers flowing through their veins. Rangers Football Club is magical and much of that is because it has the best fans in the world.

The biggest highlight of my time at Rangers has been my relationship with the fans. The fans mean so much to me and I love that I mean a lot to them as well. As I explained earlier, there was never any doubt in my mind which of the big two clubs in Scotland I wanted to play for – this obviously endeared me to the Rangers support from the off.

My first experience of the Rangers support came in that pre-season tour of Austria. The fact that a good few hundred Rangers fans had travelled there to watch their team in a friendly told me everything I needed to know about their passion for this football club. As I have documented in this book, despite settling at the club fairly quickly, I didn't have the greatest start to my first season and eventually dropped to the bench by the time we visited my previous club, Dundee. Whilst I still enjoy a great relationship with the Dundee fans, I came in for a bit of stick that day, as I have recalled elsewhere. But after coming off the bench and scoring twice I really began to find my feet and the reaction and support of the Rangers fans that day was so important to me.

The relationship with those same fans has probably defined my whole time with the club. There are far too many good stories to tell of the Rangers support and me so I will not begin to attempt to do so. However, some have stuck out for me more than most.

At various times throughout my career at Rangers I have found myself either injured, out of the picture or not selected for the squad. On all of these occasions I have become a fan myself and decided to follow follow wherever my teammates have been playing. From driving to games myself when out of the picture under Paul Le Guen to more recently going to games with one of my closest friends, I have always endeavoured to be there to see the team play. Many players try to relax and don't travel to watch the team if they are not involved and I understand why they do so but I just prefer to be there with the supporters when I can.

I remember when I was queuing for the Rangers end at

Parkhead one day and the next thing I knew I was on someone's shoulders being carried to the front of the queue with all the fans singing my name. I have been to Parkhead quite often to sit with the fans and not all my experiences are as memorable as that one!

As a player you always get an allocation of tickets. In the 2008/09 season I was injured for the second visit of the season to Celtic and was on crutches. I decided to go to the game with Donna, Ross, Donna's dad and her uncle. I also wanted to sit with one of my close friends who goes to every game. He phoned me a few days before the game to check where my seats were. When I told him he simply started laughing – the club's tickets were high up at the back of the top tier and right next to the area of segregation.

I could just imagine me climbing all the way up there on my crutches to take my seat feet away from the Celtic fans! So my friend managed to swap some tickets about and get me, Donna and Ross next to him in the corner, right in the heart of the Rangers end. I met up with him on the morning of the game and he offered to take me to the game. I decided against it and we went with Donna's dad.

On our way we got held up in traffic and ended up being dropped off at the Rangers end whilst Donna's dad went to try and park the car. We eventually made it into the stand and when I finally heard from Donna's dad, the news was not good – the car was parked in the Celtic end! My friend tried to convince me to leave with him and his group and squeeze into his car and he'd get us home. Naively I rejected the offer and waited in the Rangers end once the game had finished. I waited until the crowd had cleared then I realised that there was no way out now and I had got myself into a bit of a hairy situation!

Not for the first time, the Rangers support came to my rescue. Some members of the Galashiels loyal were in the disabled parking section of the stadium and obviously had to wait on crowds clearing before they could exit. So there we were, squeezing into the back of a people carrier heading for Galashiels! I was very lucky those guys were there that day and they drove me to a supermarket car park where my friend met us and gave me a run home! After that I took the advice of my close friend and went to any away game with him in his car rather than take chances on my own!

There have simply been so many amazing memories for me during my time with the club.

Florence will live with me forever and seeing the emotion on the faces of some of the club's sponsors, especially the guys I know well, who followed the club all over Europe that season (and every other one) made it extra special. I was honoured to be part of the squad that made these people so happy. It still disappoints me that we didn't have enough left in us to win them the UEFA Cup. Any club that can mobilise a support of 200,000 people for a game deserves that kind of success. However, I don't think any club will ever match the support that occasion brought us.

As I write this, the thought that I may no longer play for these magnificent fans does seem to cross my mind more and more often. We are, at the time of writing, still coming down from the high of winning the League Cup. I think our performance at Hampden back in March, when we beat St Mirren 1-0 after being reduced to nine men, just sums the current

Rangers squad up. We never know when we are beaten. The hunger and desire is amazing. I hope we can go on to deliver the SPL title again for the fans and that I finish the season with another League Winners medal to add to the seven medals I have right now. Whenever I finish playing football I want to look back on all the medals I've won and all the memories I cherish from this career.

However, as everyone knows, football can be a funny game and there's always speculation and uncertainty about the future. Once again there are a number of clubs interested in my signature, from Spain and some other countries in Europe but the only contract I really want to sign is with Rangers. I'd pledge my future to the club anytime in a heartbeat. But at the moment the economic uncertainty with the club makes it difficult to know what will happen in the future, both for me and other players. I just hope everything gets resolved soon so that Rangers can go on to deliver more and more success for the fans in the future.

Whatever happens, it has been an absolute honour and privilege to play for the most successful club in the world. The fans have been excellent with me, always encouraging and supporting me and I genuinely feel like I am one of them. This club is unique and ask any foreign player, such as Jorg Albertz or Arthur Numan, what this club means to them and it's clear there is a magical element to Rangers Football Club that means it's simply unlike any other.

I'm proud to say that no matter what happens in the future, I'll always be a Ranger and no one can take that away from me. I may not have been born a Ranger, nor manufactured a Ranger but like a true Ranger I understand and I need no explanation. Hopefully I've served this famous club well and I've stayed true to the values and principles that make this club and its fans the best in the world. We truly are the people.

NACHO NOVO
SENIOR CAREER STATS
(At 29 March 2010)

SD HUESCA

Season 2000/01 38 appearances 22 goals

RAITH ROVERS

Season 2001/02 38 appearances 22 goals

DUNDEE

Season 2002/03 43 appearances 9 goals

Season 2003/04 44 appearances 25 goals

RANGERS

Season 2004/05 48 appearances 25 goals

Season 2005/06 32 appearances 3 goals

Season 2006/07 39 appearances 9 goals

Season 2007/08 49 appearances 16 goals

Season 2008/09 38 appearances 9 goals

Season 2009/10 41 appearances 8 goals

CLUB TOTAL 371 APPEARANCES 126 GOALS

NATIONAL TEAM

Galicia: 2 appearances 2 goals

HONOURS

SPL CHAMPIONSHIP: 2005, 2009

SCOTTISH CUP: 2008, 2009

SCOTTISH LEAGUE CUP: 2005, 2008, 2010